HOW TO DIE IN PARIS

A MEMOIR

NATURI THOMAS

SEAL PRESS

HOW TO DIE IN PARIS
A Memoir

Copyright © 2011 by Naturi Thomas

Published by
Seal Press
A Member of the Perseus Books Group
1700 Fourth Street
Berkeley, California

Library of Congress Cataloging-in-Publication Data

Thomas, Naturi, 1974-
How to die in Paris : a memoir / by Naturi Thomas.
    p. cm.
Includes bibliographical references and index.
ISBN-13: 978-1-58005-364-8 (alk. paper)
ISBN-10: 1-58005-364-5 (alk. paper)
1. Thomas, Naturi, 1974- 2. Thomas, Naturi, 1974- —Travel—France—Paris. 3. Americans—France—Paris—Biography. 4. African American women—France—Paris—Biography. 5. Homeless women—France—Paris—Biography. 6. Paris (France)—Social conditions. 7. Mothers and daughters—United States—Biography. I. Title.
DC718.A44T46 2011
305.48'96073044361092—dc22
[B]
                    2011006583

9 8 7 6 5 4 3 2 1

Cover and interior design by Domini Dragoone
Printed in the United States of America
Distributed by Publishers Group West

DEDICATION:

TO
PARIS

CONTENTS

PART ONE

*"When one realizes his life is worthless,
he either commits suicide or travels."*

—Edward Dahlberg
"Reasons of the Heart" (*On Futility*)

PROLOGUE

When you're on the streets, you search the ground for a miracle: euros tangled in the plastic bags and newspapers left on the street, a wallet dropped under a bench, a huge wad, thousands maybe, abandoned beneath the bushes in a park by some mobster... anything that will just let you go home.

I arrive in Paris, via Italy, on the fourth of October, 2004. The newspapers I peer at through the shop windows tell me it's October still. It feels like I've been here forever, with no money, no one to turn to, and no place to call home, save the rainy autumn streets.

These are the things that I carry with me in my knapsack: a pink paisley binder stuffed with all my important papers, two books on teaching English, three paperbacks I've already read, a notebook, a pen, all the things that would fit into neither the large suitcase nor the duffel bag that is waiting for me (hopefully) in the dorm room of my ex-lover Asad.

The bag is heavy, but Asad reasoned that if I left without taking anything, I'd regret it and come back to haunt him. As he spoke, he looked right through me, as though already, I were a ghost.

"Take the knapsack," said the beautiful boy who'd rescued me from the streets, who'd tossed me back onto the streets. "Take that bag or take it all."

MEMORIES OF MY childhood chase me as I wander through Paris, through grand boulevards and shadowed back alleys alike— particularly memories of the parents I haven't spoken to in more than two years. Are my constant recollections of the past serving to distract me from my desperate situation, or is it just the madeleines they gave us passengers on the train ride over?

Or maybe anyone all alone in a strange country would get a little homesick. Even if the people who were your first home were the ones who made you sick in the first place.

GOODBYE TO ALL THAT

CH. 01

L eaving the country to start a new life is like getting to attend your own funeral: Everyone says nice things and tries not to cry. You look at all the faces at your bon voyage party, and the love for you is so visible, you could reach out and touch it.

Actually, I had more than one send-off. A few months before I left, I was part of an amateur production of *The Vagina Monologues,* along with a large cast of crazy, caring women. We liked each other so much, we started having regular cast reunions a week after the show ended. Right before I left, we went out for dinner and they toasted my future in Europe, dubbing me a "Brave Vagina." My gay friends took me dancing and attempted a futile, last-ditch effort to teach me how to walk in heels. My writing group took me out for a night of karaoke and shots. The bar, a popular after-work spot in Midtown's Little Korea, was still packed a few minutes before closing, and I hadn't gotten a chance to sing.

"Try and get the owner to bump you up on the list," the group egged me on. "Tell 'em you're leaving the country."

I stumbled up to the mike and pleaded with the people who were next on the list, "Please, I have to have a chance to sing because, um…I'm dying!" The song I chose was "No More Tears."

When she heard I was leaving, my fifty-five-year-old friend, Ginnie, dragged me to a psychic near Christopher Street. It was a boiling afternoon in early summer, but we got off the subway early to walk the last half-mile downtown. That way, I could soak up the sight of the winding streets, the cafés and quirky shops, of the West Village.

"This is one of the parts of the city I'll miss the most," I confessed to Ginnie. "Here and SoHo—they always make me think of Europe."

"What do you need to think of Europe for, silly?" Ginnie huffed beside me, dabbing her face with a handkerchief. "In a few weeks, you're going to be there!"

Her words made me anxious. I'd felt that way all week, ever since I'd emptied my savings and bought the cheapest ticket to Florence I could find.

"Twenty dollars for a ten-minute reading!" I exploded when we got outside the psychic's. I showed Ginnie the time on my watch. "Isn't it a little irresponsible to be blowing forty dollars on some charlatan when it's happy hour?"

Ginnie, a hip former hippie who wore her grey hair long and unashamedly down her back, was one of my best drinking buddies. This time, however, she didn't bite.

"It's my treat, of course. Even if you don't believe in anything, I do, and I want to make sure you'll be safe," she said, then added, " I don't want to lose you, too."

I almost protested again, until I remembered that Ginnie had lost her husband to a heart attack, and one son to a heroin overdose; another son, a troubled teen she'd adopted had just disappeared.

"I believe in stuff!" I retorted, as we opened the door and macheted our arms through the love beads. "Not this, necessarily, but I do believe in *something*. It's hardly my fault," I added, "if the feeling isn't mutual."

The psychic's salon was in a dim, cluttered storefront that seemed to double as her apartment. A TV whispered in a back room. As Ginnie and I fanned ourselves in the poorly ventilated waiting area, a little girl skipped out from the back, threw us an uncurious glance, and shouted toward a closed door leading off to the side: "Hey, Ma, where's my report card?"

"I'm with a customer!" came the hissed response from behind the door. "And anyway, how should I know?"

I shot Ginnie a look. "This should be good."

When it was my turn, the psychic led me to a red velvet room, gestured for me to sit in a red velvet chair, and wound an egg timer on the table. Her hand, holding my palm upward, was limp.

"Your friend says you are here to make a long journey," she intoned, in a voice completely different from the one she had used with her kid, "and a mere glance at your lines tells me she is correct. It will be hard for you at first, but in the end, you will be okay." The psychic barely stifled a yawn. Suddenly, her eyes widened and she reached for a pair of cheap reading glasses.

"Actually, it will be very, very hard at first." She began holding my palm up closer and closer to her face. "Extremely, terribly hard. I mean, really—"

"Thanks!" I snatched my hand away. "I get it."

THEY DID EVERYTHING for me, the people in my life, except ask me why I was leaving in the first place. Why had I cleared out my tiny, bouncy checking account to relocate to a place where I had no job, knew not a single soul, and most likely would be unable to watch season six of *The Sopranos*?

If they had, I wouldn't have been able to tell them.

A few months before I left for Paris, I called a suicide hotline. I'd been watching daytime TV, searching for a sign. What should I do with my life? Train to be a mechanic in six weeks? A dental assistant in two? Sue someone? Then I saw the toll-free number to the Sunshine House and called before the ad ended.

"Good morning, Sunshine, please hold."

Good, that gave me time to think. What, exactly, was wrong? I was afraid of people's eyes, afraid of setting off the sensors in bookstores when I hadn't stolen anything, afraid of fucking unless I was drunk, afraid that police sirens in the distance were for me. My boyfriend was married. My two best friends, who worked in retail, said things like "Purple is the new black" in hushed, reverent tones. I hadn't talked to my parents in two years, and no one in the family—not my grandpa, my aunts, my uncle, or even my younger brother, Stewie—had ever asked why. One morning, I'd twisted and twisted the pole on the blinds in my bedroom, trying to get them tight enough so that they wouldn't let in a bit of sun. The pole had come off in my hands.

Ten minutes later, the girl came back on the line. "Uh, like, thanks for holding. Listen, we're a little backed up right now. Do you think we could take your number and call you back? Or is this an emergency?"

"Oh, no, nothing's wrong at all," I assured her, before hanging up. "I was just checking to see if you guys were okay."

THE DAY OF my flight, my friend Meena helped me move my computer, my TV, and most of my other possessions into storage, then drove me to JFK. Meena was stylish and sassy. She came from one of those super-religious Muslim families in which the girl has to be a virgin on her wedding night ... or else.

"You have to sleep with all the men I can't," Meena instructed me. She ran down the list: a French guy with pouty lips and a goatee; a hot gondolier in Venice who wore one of those striped turtlenecks; a Spanish flamenco dancer in tight pants.

"What about a Muslim guy?" I teased her.

"Promise me," Meena said sternly, "you won't do that."

While waiting in line at the airport check-in, we saw a woman and a little girl kiss a businessman goodbye. The man started off with his luggage, when suddenly the little girl ran after him, flinging herself on the man's legs. "Please, Daddy! Don't leave me! Stay with me, Daddy! Please!" The man and the woman looked at each other helplessly. Meena pulled out her cell and made a call, allowing us both to pretend that she didn't notice that I had started to cry, too.

ROAMIN' HOLIDAY

CH. 02

M y trip to Europe that summer wasn't the first time I'd been out of the country. Once, when I was in grade school, my parents decided on a whim to take us on a road trip to a famous historical district in Canada. We were fine until we crossed the border. Then my father got us so lost that even my mother started asking, "Are we *there* yet?" Finally, it got so late that we grabbed dinner at a McDonald's and collapsed at a Howard Johnson.

A few years later, during a visit to San Diego, my grandpa took my little brother and me across the border to Tijuana, Mexico. We followed him around the open-air markets with our hands practically shellacked to our sides, due to his frequent injunctions to Not. Touch. *Anything.* Lunch that day: Denny's.

But Florence was a dream. My flight got in too late to allow me to do any more than find my hostel and collapse in the only free bed in my shared room. That next morning, however, I left to go find something for breakfast and ended up wandering about until dark. Love, success, contentment—everything in life had eluded me thus far, but this was the Europe I'd always dreamed of. I walked slowly down the winding, ancient streets, a lump in my throat, as though down the aisle at my own wedding.

It wasn't long before I befriended two of the girls with whom I shared a room. Jackie was plump, cynical, and hilarious. Helena, her best friend, was a thin, dreamy girl who grew helpless with laughter whenever Jackie pronounced some withering critique of the nude statues we walked past. "She's *mental,* int' she?" Helena would nudge me. "She's absolutely *mad!*" They'd grown up together in a village in England that was so quaint, it still had a milkman. I made them tell me everything about it and tried not to think too often of home.

The medieval Old Town was a little too dark and dingy for the girls, but I loved everything we saw: the public gardens lush with wildflowers and silent nooks, the views of the city from the hills, and the street performers in the piazzas, where the crowds watched impromptu shows while hugging their knapsacks and purses, less from excitement than to protect themselves from gypsies.

There were also cute, tiny grandmas, gorgeous women gunning down the cobblestone streets on their Vespas, and nuns, traveling in twos and threes, who lingered in front of shop window displays of killer-looking leather boots.

I didn't notice any men; I wouldn't let myself. I'd just suffered a wrenching breakup with my boyfriend of almost a year, after discovering he was afraid of commitment—which came as kind of a shock, him being married and all. This, however, turned out to be perfect timing. I'd been reading a lot of articles on the practice of celibacy, how it enabled people, especially women, to focus on their work, their purpose in life. I didn't let the fact that I had neither a calling nor an actual job weaken my resolve.

My new friends and I all agreed on the most beautiful thing about Italy: In the supermarkets, you could get a big box of table wine for less than the cost of a cup of coffee. *Less than the cost of a cup of coffee.* Everything I knew about choosing a fine bottle went out the window the afternoon I learned this, along with the itinerary of gallery hopping the girls and I had planned for the day. We returned to the hostel, each lugging a bag of wine boxes. By evening, we were not only smashed but also starving, since, once we'd seen the wine at the market, we'd forgotten to get any actual food.

We stumbled arm in arm in arm down crowded Via Cavour. Tourists, glancing up from their maps, jumped out of the way just in time. The locals wove around us with practiced ease, throwing us annoyed but well-dressed looks.

"God, what I wouldn't do for a bit of fish and chips," Jackie fretted. Her head swiveled from left to right as she steered us past the delicious scents coming from a line of restaurants. "You know, my dad *said* there were no pubs in Italy. I thought he was just trying to frighten me...."

I hung back a moment to glance at a menu posted outside a café. When I looked up, the girls had disappeared. I hurried through the crowd, finally spotting them in front of a gelato stand across the street. No sooner had I stepped into the road than the car approaching screeched to a stop not six inches away from me.

I'm not sure what the car's exact make was, but it was the type for which commercials are shot in black and white, in which the car is shown zooming about some pristine locale while its virtues are expounded by a narrator with a voice like God.

There was a man inside. He had a well-kept mane of black hair, eyes that pierced through the glass. There are no words in the English language that could come close to describing the effect his mouth, curling into a half-smile, had on me.

I noticed his cuff links when he lifted his big hands from his steering wheel. These he turned into pistols, which he fired at me one by one in lazy, amused reproach. His mouth formed the words "boom-boom."

I made an apologetic gesture, than walked in a daze across the street, where the girls were waiting for me. One look at my face, and Helena held out her gelato to me.

"Did you guys just see that? *Don't look!*" I shrieked, as the car turned the corner near us and went down a side street. The girls, standing as though they were frozen from the neck down in blocks of ice, followed it with just their eyes.

"So what? You almost got run over by a really posh car," Jackie shrugged. "Well done."

"No, I'm talking about the man *in* the car. Remember back in the room today, when I was telling you guys about my past relationships, and how I never want to date again?" They nodded.

"Well, maybe it's not that I didn't want to fall in love again; it's that I thought I couldn't, that some vital part of me had been broken. Well, I guess I was wrong." I shook my head. "You should've seen that guy. I coulda dated the hell out of him."

The girls were swaying a bit, leaning against each other for support as they listened to me. When I finished, Helena lurched forward, throwing her arms around me. She got the majority of her gelato in my hair. Jackie, who, I noticed for the first time, had forgotten to put on her shoes, patted my arm approvingly.

"Thash beautiful," she said.

A FEW DAYS later, I bid arrivederci to the girls. Having fled the latte-fueled psychosis of Manhattan, I was reluctant to settle in, or near, another urban center. I dreamed of starting over again in some pictur-esque rural European village, just like in *Under the Tuscan Sun* or *A Year in Provence*. On my way to market each morning, my bike would bounce along cobblestone streets; I'd make lots of friends and we'd sit around my rustic wood table, spitting olive pits and laughing.

Two things I hadn't considered:

1) There aren't many jobs in tiny, picturesque villages, particularly for foreigners who don't speak the language and have no work visa or any marketable skills whatsoever.

2) The authors of those books were white. Unless you count my mother (who was black), my encounters with racism had been few.

At least, that is, until I hit the Boot. No one ever said anything to me, unless you count their eyes.

Or maybe it wasn't racism; I was just Something Different. And if you live in a little hamlet where there's a better chance of a rooster crossing your path than of seeing a person who looks different from what you're used to, you stare. I, for one, stared at the four or five roosters I encountered on my southern Italian rambles. Stared at them unblinkingly, not smiling when they looked my way. Maybe I made *them* feel bad. Perhaps one of those roosters had grown up hearing the word "chicken" as a pejorative in his own house, was constantly made to feel like something was wrong with him. Now he wandered, looking for a place he could call home. He watched townsfolk greet each other at the market and the old women gossiping out their windows as they hung their whites on the line. Perhaps, after a solitary dinner at a café, that rooster walked the winding back streets until he caught sight of a family gathered around the dinner table: the clink of cutlery, the plates passed into waiting hands, voices rising and falling in a language he slowly began to realize he was never going to learn from any guidebook.

Or maybe I'm projecting.

Either way, I spent days in idyllic seaside towns south of Naples and lovely burgs around Siena, pretending that people were stopping in the middle of the street and staring at me because I was a rock star. Then I got sick of touring and went to Rome.

ONE STORMY AFTERNOON when I was four, I found my mother smiling as she gazed out the living room window, as if the thunder and wind were singing a song just for her. It was dim in the apartment, much quieter than outside. My dad had just lost his job and was keeping out of my mother's way—not easy in our tiny two-bedroom. My two-year-old brother was sitting in his playpen, engaged in a daylong bout of watching the wall like it was the Super Bowl playoffs, a hobby that would have caused most parents to consult a specialist but that, according to my mom, meant he was simply "so much easier than his fucking sister."

His fucking sister was bored. To my surprise, my mother's smile didn't fade as I approached the window and tapped at her leg.

"Whatcha lookin' at, Ma?" She drew back the curtain and showed me the day. Leaves and branches ringed-around-the-rosy in the wind. Ribbons of lightning flashed across a sullen sky. The trees rocked and swayed, as if daring it to do its worst.

"I love this, days like this, when everything is so wild and electric. It's sexy, you know what I mean?" This was a "yes" question. I nodded.

My mother sneered, let the curtain fall into my face. "No, you don't. God, there's no one to talk to. . . . " Her gaze swept the apartment: the stiff, plaid couches, the beige dinette set, the glass-topped coffee table that, thanks to me and my yo-yo, was now glassless. Through the open door of my parents' room my father could be seen at their desk, poring over the jobs section of the newspaper, rubbing his forehead like a genie's lamp.

"Yeah I do!" I protested. "Sexy is like the Fonz."

It was a good thing, to make my mother laugh. She tugged my pigtail nicely, like she was my friend.

"Hey, I have an idea. Let's go outside. Let's take a walk in the storm."

I was already running for my sweater as I called back, "But what if it starts to rain?"

"Then we'll get wet."

The streets were empty and the world was ours. We had to shout over the wind, and I made my mother smile by pretending it was blowing me all around. Then a fantastic *smack* of thunder made us shriek like teenage girls. There was a field facing our apartment building, and all around was the smell of the earth opening, waiting to receive its due.

"We could go to the store and get stuff to have a tea party," I suggested.

"We could," my mother said, her head raised to the clouds. "Or we could get on the bus that takes us to Newark Airport and get on a plane, any plane, and leave all this shit behind."

Who could I invite to our tea party? My stomach started to feel wiggly.... My best dog, Fluffy, and Peter Piglet and Dressy Bessy.... My mother, holding my hand, walked us across the street with her eyes still on the sky.... Very Bear would have to sit next to me, since he didn't get along with anyone....

My mother slapped my hand; I was biting my nails.

It got fun again in the too-bright store, as we picked out treats and decided what we would wear once we got back home. The owner threw in a small bag of pretzels. "For the pretty little girl," he said, not taking his eyes off my mother.

Of course, the minute we stepped back outside, the skies opened upon us. We ran through ropes of rain that drenched our clothes and hair; we tried to scream, but we were laughing too hard. When we got into the building, we kept running, up the three flights of stairs, as though the storm would chase us through the door.

My father was on his hands and knees in the center of the living room, covering something grey and unspeakable with paper towels.

"I think the baby has diarrhea," my dad sighed. "He's in the tub. Don't worry, there's no water in it. Oh, and we're going to have to get a new playpen."

My mother and I turned to look at the playpen, then inched away from it.

"What's that smell?" She looked toward the kitchen.

"It's baby shit," I said helpfully.

"I started dinner." My dad looked up from the Lysol and winked. "Nothing better on a day like this than tuna casserole."

I looked up at my mother's face, the strands of wet hair still clinging to her cheeks, and I knew. I knew that by the time I'd toweled off and changed into tea-party clothes, she would have crawled into bed. And that after I set up the tea things at my play table, Bessy and Fluffy and Peter and Very Bear and I would save a chair for my mother, who would not get out of bed until morning. And that halfway through the party, Very Bear, as predicted, would be naughty, and I would have no choice but to smack him to the ground.

AN AGENCY FOUND me a job teaching English to two boys, twenty hours a week, for room, board, and something called "pocket money." I could've gotten something full-time, a position that didn't require me to live with the family. But it was so nice to have everything taken care of:

meals, clean sheets, an allowance. It was like being a child again. After three weeks of seeing Heaven on Earth and finding it closed to me, I settled for just not having to worry, not having to think very much at all.

The boys, ages five and ten, were very bright. Within a week, they had learned to say, "We hate Engleesh and we hate yooo." Then they would kick soccer balls at me. Meeting people was hard. I knew about twenty words in Italian, and eight of those were pizza toppings. I needed a friend.

Enter Donatella, the boys' mother. Petite, with birdlike movements and baby-doll eyes, she'd wave away the boys' seething hatred for the stranger whose arrival had forced them to share a room. She invited me for chats on the terrace over tiny cups of coffee. "They'll pick up English from listening to us." I forgot my own troubles as she poured out her heart out over her master's thesis, her workaholic husband, and her late mother, who'd insisted on being buried with her purse. I, in turn, regaled her with tales of the fabulous life I'd left behind in New York. They were great, my stories—total fiction. I could've written for *Sex and the City.*

Donatella seemed to agree. I was so lucky, she sighed, to have been born speaking English. It was such a difficult language to master, much less write a thesis in. Could I possibly help her?

I couldn't see why not. Sure, I had my own writing to do, the boys' lessons. Then the steady, patient work of taping the lessons together after the boys had found them and torn them to shreds. Still, I assured her, I'd be happy to do a little editing, a little troubleshooting. After all, we were friends.

The next morning, on the kitchen table, I found a monstrous Italian–English dictionary and many, many sheets of handwritten notebook paper, entitled "Structural Didactics and Physiology in Amateur Gymnastics," along with a note:

> "Please to translate this.
> *Molte grazie!*"

That afternoon, I explained to Donatella that I didn't know enough Italian to translate a 130-page thesis. Considering the topic, I probably didn't know enough English. She smiled, offered me biscotti with our usual coffee. I was a smart girl, she reassured me; I'd figure it out.

Day after day for a week, the stack of books and papers sat untouched. Coffee hour grew increasingly tense. Meanwhile, the boys had started to come around, now that I'd integrated *Grand Theft Auto* into our daily lessons. But Donatella was not pleased.

A week later, she asked me if I would help her take the boys to the pool. I liked going to the club with her. While the kids swam, I'd sit with all the moms, practicing my Italian while they plied me with questions about Amereeka. After my initial reception in Italy, the whole thing was just what I needed.

That day was to be different. Once the boys had dispersed and we were at the club café, Donatella reached into her swim bag, hauling out the dictionary and thesis. The table shook a bit as she set them down.

"I really need your help," she said quietly. "And I don't think it's too much to ask."

I explained to her that what she needed was a professional translator. The English-language bookstores I frequented were full of ads offering these services. I could help her find one; they only charged…

"No! *Basta!* I must pay for everything! The boys' school, club fees, my credit cards, the beach house…."

I quickly bandaged my heart, which had begun bleeding all over the table, and told her I was sorry, but I couldn't help her.

Donatella left me alone at the table, gathering all the other moms around her. Much multisyllabic hissing and many indignant glares in my direction for the rest of the hour. I heard the word *puttana* a few times and wondered if that meant, "Does anyone know where I can find a reasonably priced translator?"

The minute we got home, Donatella hurried toward the master bathroom, where her constipated insurance salesman of a husband spent most of his time. Thirty seconds later, he poked his head out the door and told me I was fired. The boys simply weren't learning any English. I had until the next morning to leave. (At just that moment, the younger boy ran by us, yelling, "Stop that bastardo! He steal my Porsche!")

SACKED IN ROME, I fled by train back to Florence. I remembered only how happy I'd been there, and not the fact that the hostel where I'd stayed, located in the city's center, had to be booked weeks in advance. When I arrived in Florence this time, it was on a Saturday evening at the height of tourist season. Every hostel and cheap *albergo* was booked solid. With only €150 to my name, I couldn't have afforded to stay anyplace more than a week anyway.

The thing to do at that point would've been to email everyone for help: my grandparents and brother, my ex-lover and friends. Instead, I pushed my way through the well-heeled crowds around the Uffizi and headed for the Arno. I always thought best by a river.

Couples strolled along the path by the water, at home in each other's arms. I watched the banana gelato I had bought melt onto the ground at my feet. How in the world was I supposed to tell people I had gotten fired from a job as a glorified baby sitter? That not only had I made almost no money from said job, but I'd also blown through my small life savings as well? This was partly because my last-minute ticket to Florence had cost a lot of money. Plus, I had misconstrued the dollar-to-euro exchange rate in favor of the former (how patriotic). Not helping my meager financial-planning skills was the pastel, generic appearance of paper euros. It's hard to take your money seriously when it looks like it was manufactured by Milton Bradley.

Besides, how could I ask for money to get home when there was no home to go to? I'd left an apartment I couldn't afford and a series of jobs that didn't sustain me, parents I no longer spoke to, and an extended family who pretended not to notice. Europe was supposed to be an end to the luckless grind my life had become. I'd never been abroad before; I hadn't known there was no escaping myself.

Even if I swallowed my pride and asked for help to get home, I would've had to start over. Another crappy job and dingy apartment full of roommates even more fucked up than me. Boyfriends who didn't love me and friends who didn't understand me. Not enough. It was never enough.

And then there was my family.

There was nothing left to do but die.

But of course, I'd have to spend the last of my money for a train ticket to the City of Love. Not only was it a place I'd always dreamed of, but just think about it: Go all the way to Europe, spend three months there, and then kill myself without seeing Paris first? People would think I was crazy.

A SIMPLE PLAN

CH. 03

When I first arrive in Paris, I catch a ride from Bercy station with a fellow passenger who offers to drop me at a youth hostel. In the cab, it dawns on me that I've arrived in a strange city with just enough money to last one night. That for months I'd been terrified to fall asleep and awoke each morning racked with sobs. That the only thing left for me in this life was to see Paris once, before I died. Now I stare out the window, seeing nothing.

I find a hostel in the run-down neighborhood near Gare du Nord. There is a bar on the ground floor with a great sound system. As I check in, Tracy Chapman is talkin' 'bout a revolution, Eric Clapton about cocaine. After a sleepless night on the sleeper train, realizing what I have done, I could use some of either.

"You're only staying in Paris for one night?" the receptionist asks.

"That's all I need."

I'VE BOOKED MYSELF into one of the shared rooms: two bunk beds, one bathroom, four purple walls. My three roommates burst in, fresh from a genuine French breakfast of café au lait and the best croissants, like, ever. They're from California.

"You want to come to the Louvre with us?"

I laugh. "Is it free?"

"Actually, the first Sunday of every month it is."

The Métro, round-trip, however, costs €2.80. We get on the wrong train, get off at the wrong stop, and wander for a while around bustling Rue de Rivoli. The girls buy postcards to send to their mothers, take pictures of children on a carousel at a street fair. There's a cart featuring foot-long double hot dogs covered in melted gruyère. They douse theirs in ketchup while the vendor shakes his head.

"Aren't you going to get one?" they ask.

My stomach is cramping with hunger. I have to save my money for tomorrow, though, to buy poison. "I'm good," I smile.

In the courtyard of the Louvre, during the seven years we stand in line, they tell me about their lives. Two of them go to USC and one of them goes to UC Santa Barbara. They've been friends since first grade. They've been backpacking all through Europe: London, Prague, Amsterdam. They got *soo* fucked up in Amsterdam. They're off to Spain next. Can't wait—after six weeks away from home, they're really starting to miss tacos.

"And what brings you to Paris?" they ask me.

I give them the *Reader's Digest* version. "Well, I was traveling around Italy, then I picked up some work in Rome. When the job ended, I decided I just had to come to Paris."

"How long are you staying?"

"I plan to spend the rest of my life here."

They take off their sunglasses as one, staring at me with unabashed admiration. "Wow, that's really brave."

One of the girls looks around the courtyard of the Louvre—at the wide stone buildings, the glass pyramids glittering in the sun. "Everybody should see Paris before they die," she says.

MY LUCKY NIGHT

CH. 04

THIS IS WHAT I wear on my last day alive: dark blue jeans, red argyle sweater, socks with the smallest holes.

THIS IS ALL the money I have left in the world: €6.03.

THIS IS WHAT I carry in my knapsack: diary to record last thoughts for posterity, pen and loose-leaf paper for suicide letter, paperback novel to finish quickly.

THIS IS THE plan: buy poison, then take it, then die.

AT THE HOSTEL, I leave behind the bulk of my luggage—a giant suitcase full of books, a duffel bag full of clothes. This morning, as I returned my key to the front desk, I asked if there was a place I could leave my bags for a day or two. The staff pointed me toward the basement storage, used temporarily by guests who were checking out but unsure of their next destination.

I guessed that would be me.

What I do know is that I need to get to the Eiffel Tower. When I ask for directions, one of the staff members takes out a map of the Métro and marks with a pen the quickest route to the tower. A few guests hanging out at the bar tell me to be sure to check out the Latin Quarter. This sparks a friendly debate between the guests and the front-desk clerk about that neighborhood's best café. Out of habit, I jot down a few of their suggestions on my map. When I thank them, they tell me they wish they were going to see the tower for the very first time. They sound so sincere that I feel lucky as I step outside, blinking against the morning light. Then I remember the reason I'm here, and that it's the last time I will ever blink against the morning light. There's no room for anything else in my head. I try as hard as I can to make sense of my mapped route. Then I set out in exactly the opposite direction.

A scant eleven hours later, I am standing before the Eiffel Tower, knees shaking with awe. I knew the tower was tall; I didn't know it was *that* tall. I've seen pictures of it lit up at night.

I didn't know that bitch sparkled.

The evening is warm, and the park in front of the tower has the air of an outdoor concert. Groups of people sit on blankets, drinking, playing guitars. Vendors hawking beer and little glow-in-the-dark

Eiffels mill through the crowd. I find an empty patch of grass and settle down to think.

My quest for poison has not been successful. I haven't been able to find anything lethal in the supermarkets, there are only cosmetics in the pharmacies, and the French don't seem to have any hardware stores. Walking by the many florists, I remembered the warning on packets of flower food I used to get with my bouquets in New York. Then I thought of someone killing himself with flower food. It was actually pretty funny. I was actually pretty funny. To reward myself, I bought a pack of cigarettes.

The means of my undoing are not the only thing I seek. During my long walk toward death, I was just as I'd been during my walk through life. Lost. Looking for a sign. The closer I got, when I began to see the top of the tower framed against the clouds, the more desperate my thoughts grew. If I could figure out how I'd gotten to this place, could I also figure a way out?

My mind takes refuge in the past, replaying the last few months, until I have to face the disconcerting fact that I may have gone to Florence in the first place only because my boyfriend went there the summer before. With his wife, not me. Though he told me endless stories of how great it was, he didn't bring anything back for me. I understood, of course—probably a little hard to get a knicknack for your mistress while hanging out with your wife. Maybe part of the reason I felt the need to get away at all was that, after months of increasing closeness, he suddenly became distant, sullen as a teenage boy. When I confronted him, he said it was because he couldn't allow himself to love me.

Even though I broke up with him, for some reason I understood that, too.

But there is still so much that I don't get. In the past, I read every story about suicide I could lay my hands on, often wondered about the one question those stories couldn't answer: What do people think right before death, when their death lies in their own hands? Is there a whisper in the brain that takes the fear away? Some insight as to why life, for them at least, had to be so much more than they could bear? The last part is what I've been hoping for especially. My life has never made sense to me, not from the beginning. Shouldn't I at least find out what I did to deserve it at the end?

But me, I'm just thinking stupid stuff. Like, *What if someone reads my diary? . . . I'll never have another first kiss. . . . I'll never have that conversation with a soon-to-be friend where we find out we have so much in common ("You like pizza? I like pizza, too!"). . . . I'll never be at the beach, shrieking as I run across the hot sand into the cool sea.*

But I'm being silly. Like it or not, I have to kill myself. I have no money, no way of calling for help or getting myself home. I have, in fact, cut off all avenues of escape, knowing that I'd flee down any left open. I'm not going to kill myself out of revenge or to show them all, and it certainly isn't a cry for help. Crying, I've learned, almost never helps.

It's just that my life is a house on fire. It's been burning for so long. I have to get out. I have to.

I decide to just throw myself off the Eiffel Tower. Now that's class. Problem is, as far as I can see, the whole structure is encased in glass. It costs anywhere from €10 to €15 to get in, and now I have only 53¢. (I've bought a Coke, too.) Also, I'm a bit leery of heights. From where I sit in front of the tower, fewer than forty feet away, I'm afraid to look all the way up, much less scale it and fling myself from the top.

I shut my eyes against the glittering lights. I can't even kill myself right. All around me, people are laughing, singing along to a strummed guitar. Couples snuggle and kiss on blankets. Every time someone walks by me, I freeze. I'm always like that in public places, afraid that someone will make me move, that I don't have the right to be where I am. A couple of guys circle; I am the only woman alone. A vendor hunkers down a few feet away and stares. A guy in glasses limps back and forth behind me. I keep my eyes fixed on the tower, and the people fade away. I smoke cigarette after cigarette. Some kid comes up and offers me fifty cents for one. I give it to him, but I can never take money, even if it would boost my income by half. I wonder how long it'll take to starve to death.

THE DAY I was born, my mother decided I needed to be taught a lesson. Despite the instructions on my chart, a nurse accidentally gave me a bottle for my first feeding. At the next, I turned my face away from the breast with a resolve that the staff found amusing. My mother did not. Determined to feed me her way, she instructed the nurses, "Just give me another hour." Each time, I was brought to her screaming with hunger, only to turn away with my lips clamped shut. Amid the confusion of shift changes and the general chaos of the maternity ward at Los Angeles County General Hospital, I was not fed until almost eight hours later. My father arrived at the hospital after work to find me nearly a pound lighter than when I'd first been pushed out into the world. I was bottle-fed from then on.

My mother told me this story throughout my life, sometimes jokingly, sometimes in rebuke, always with the cap "See, right from the start, you were trouble."

I liked to think of it more as: The first battle I ever had with my mother, I won.

ANOTHER GUY. THIS time, I'm not even going to look. He's seated himself nearby, facing me, rather than the tower. That's bold. Doesn't matter—all losers are.

I haven't eaten for more than twenty-four hours. After a day spent walking around the entire city, my stomach is so hollow that the growls echo. I figure that by this time two days from now, I'll be dead. I think of a snack in Italy called *fritti*: balls of potato covered with a spicy sauce-and-rice mixture, then fried within an inch of their lives. Tiny *pastini* smothered in meatballs and marinara, sausage that sends juice trickling down your chin, a hot square of pizza *margherita* fresh from the oven....

"*Buona sera.*"

At the look on my face, the guy shakes his head. "*Pardon, pardon-moi.*"

"No, I speak Italian."

He sits, folding his long legs beneath him in the grass. "How do you speak Italian?" he asks me in Italian.

I give him the same story I gave the girls at the Louvre. It's hard to lie in another language. As I search for the words, I'm checking him out: dark hair, pretty mouth, nice body. I interrupt myself, leaning forward. "Are your eyes green?"

He laughs. I recoil. He goes, "Eh-eh-eh-eh." Like a sheep with a sore throat. Still, he's fine. And what luck, finding a guy who speaks Italian in Paris! Maybe I haven't come here to die. Maybe I've come here to meet . . .

"What did you say your name was, again?"

Frankie is from a village near Naples, has come to Paris to find work. He lives just a few blocks away.

We have two beers each and kiss ravenously in the kiddie park nearby. The tower sparkles in the empty bottles at our feet.

Frankie doesn't exactly have his own apartment; he stays with a friend. You can see the Eiffel Tower from the bathroom, he tells me, pressing the buzzer. He has the key to the front door, but not the apartment itself. He buzzes again. I yawn in the silence.

"*Aspett'*. Wait here—no problem." He kisses me, then bounds up the stairs. He comes down a minute later, slowly.

"He's got a girl up there," he tells me, his lips tight.

"Well, can't we just go in your room and stay there?"

Frankie doesn't exactly have his own room. Eh-eh-eh.

"Then where do you . . . ?"

"Not too many questions. I know a place." He takes me by the hand. He seems to know exactly where he's going. I let my eyes close as we walk.

Frankie makes me hop a night bus, though neither of us has a ticket and I'm scared of the controllers who board the bus and make random checks, scared of the loud group of guys, seated in the back, passing a bottle of wine. The bus lumbers past the Pont de l'Alma, angels glittering in the night. We turn down *rue* after twisting *rue* of cheese shops and dress shops and buildings with balconies like black lace. Then the streets grow wider, with chicken places and sullen-looking men on each corner. After about thirty minutes, we get off. It's colder. The wind blows garbage toward us, and no matter what direction I look, I can't see the tower.

"Where are we?"

"St. Denis."

"Is St. Denis part of Paris?"

"No, it's St. Denis." I open my mouth to protest. "My uncle lives here; he can give us money." He takes my hand. "But first we need a bed."

The night clerk at the hotel has a long face and eyes that say, *This is not what I wanted to be when I grew up.* As we approach, I turn to Frankie in time to see him hunch his shoulders. He lets go of my hand to dig around in his pocket.

"My passport," he says, sliding it across the desk. "Please, *signor*—I mean, *monsieur*—I will go get the money from my uncle in the morning."

Mais non, it's not possible! If his boss comes early to check the books.... The man pantomimes a limp gun to his head, then pulls the trigger.

"But I will get up very early and get the money from him then. They let me do it at the other place." He points to the hotel we tried initially, which is boarded up.

"I'm sorry. I need the money up front."

"But it's four in the morning; my uncle is sleeping."

"*Alors,* if you want to be as well, *monsieur,* you had better go and wake him."

Three blocks of broken glass, a long wait in the run-down corridor of his uncle's flat. Frankie's knock on the door is timorous but determined. I hide in the shadows. Finally, the door opens a crack. "I need fifty euros." My hero's voice sounds surprisingly high. The door closes. That's okay. I could sleep right here, on the unfinished floor. It's just as cold as outside, but the wind has stopped chasing us.

Finally, the door opens. *Plop.* Two twenties and a ten, balled up, land at Frankie's feet. This time, the door slams. I move away a little, rustling in my bag. It's dark in the corridor and easy to pretend I don't see how he must get down on all fours and pat the ground to find the money.

Outside, Frankie links his arm through mine, laughing at the way I sway each time a wave of wind hits me.

"You're tired." He kisses my forehead.

"Is your uncle nice?"

"He's the best, *molto bravo.*" He squeezes my arm, then, thinking better of it, my ass.

In the hotel, there's a sink behind a curtain where I can freshen up, watch as his clothing hits the floor, one piece at a time. Frankie fucks like he hasn't in a long while, moves like he's trying to outrun the fact of being a man with no money, who sleeps on a couch only when his friend lets him in. I dig my nails into his back like it's the edge of the cliff he's just saved me from.

"You're going to stay with me. I'll take care of you." This is what he says afterward, or maybe I dream it. When I open my eyes, he is already snoring into my hair.

THINGS
FALL
APART

CH. 05

I awaken the next afternoon feeling shaky and scared. It's as if I've had a sudden, brutal illness that left me as quickly as it came. One false move, and it'll return.

I lie on my back, Frankie's arm thrown around my neck. I cling to it, searching for the face of God on the water-stained walls.

Tell me what I should do now.

Sometimes it's the cover of night that reveals the most. Not only am I a fuckup, I'm also a coward. Instead of sticking to the only plan that made sense, I allowed my final hour to devolve into happy hour. All I've done is delay the inevitable.

Or have I? I stand up, walk across the room to throw open the papery curtains. My limbs feel slow and flu-weak. Sunlight pours into the room, bathing them in warmth.

WE HAVE ONLY half an hour before our one o'clock checkout, so I dress quickly, then rouse Frankie. He has his face in the pillow and keeps shifting to give me one-eyed glares, but I'm terrified of staying even one minute over, imagining an irate manager pounding on the door, standing over us as we gather our things. Back in the States, I had to move sixteen times in the last six years. If I've learned one thing, it's that it's always better to leave than to be kicked out.

After a second fuck and a cigarette, my new lover perks up. He takes me to one of the Turkish kebab places that are all over Europe. He orders a huge pita, overstuffed with shards of meat sliced from a giant spit, along with lettuce, tomato, and some of the best fries I've ever had. I'm thirsty, but he says we can't afford a Coke. Not that we'll be poor for much longer—Frankie has plans for us.

Do I like babies? His cousin has one, and she needs someone to watch it. A gorgeous little boy, looks a lot like Frankie. His cousin's husband travels a lot, and she likes to party while he's away. They live in the ritzy Invalides section of Paris. I could sleep there on the couch while he finds an apartment for us, a job of his own.

After my au pair stint in Italy, the thought of living in another woman's house, being at her mercy, is enough to make me want to run out the door, leaving behind the only food I've had in almost two days and the person who may be my only chance to survive.

To distract myself, I imagine my own children, the ones Frankie and I could have. They'd be ravishing: with his eyes, hopefully; my laugh, definitely. I also decide he'd look much better in dark slacks and button-downs than in the baggy jeans and sweatshirt he now sports. Didn't he say he'd done a lot of construction work back in Italy? He could open his own contracting business here and be madly successful. I would stay home with the children. Our house would be very warm.

"Wait right here. I'm going to see if she's home." I stand outside the call center, absorbing St. Denis in all its daytime glory. It's started to rain, and immigrants from various Third World countries hurry down the street with carriages or laundry carts, flagging down a bus that's about to pull off. The garbage cans overflow and the buildings look peeled and faded. In the time it takes me to smoke a cigarette, no fewer than five men try to bum one off me. These people are not much different than I am— outsiders struggling with survival and the ever-rising cost of a pack of smokes. They are just like me, actually, and I hate them.

Frankie comes out, shaking his head. "*Non è a la sua casa.*" We start walking. "Right now I want to see if my other cousin is home. Maybe he'll let us stay on the couch in his place."

"Is his place in Paris?"

"Nope, five blocks away." He makes a gay gesture that ends with his arm around me, pulls me close to kiss me on the cheek.

"Do you know anyone else who lives in Paris where we can stay?" He looks hurt; my cheek has been unresponsive.

"Why, what's wrong? It's not dangerous here."

When I was fourteen, we finally managed to move from the inner city to the suburbs. My life upon leaving my parents' house, however, became once again a succession of dirty streets, ugly buildings, and people who couldn't even wait to step out of line at the corner store before they started scratching their lottery tickets. My two days in

Paris have shown me wide boulevards and elegant little shops; women who know what to do with a scarf; and men in berets, biking home, a loaf of crusty bread under one arm—a world I longed for before I even knew it existed.

Frankie grabs my hand. "Come on, don't be that way. Things will work out. It'll only be for a little while."

His eyes search my face. I smile at him. He's right. It doesn't matter. He's a good guy. I don't know what's wrong with me. When I say this, he dashes into a corner store. Comes out with a Coke.

I AM PLANTED in a nearby park, instructed to wait five minutes, ten tops. A group of ragged men are eating bread and kicking at the pigeons who've gathered at their feet. When Frankie sees them eyeing me, he eyes them back, kisses me long and territorially goodbye. I decide I love him.

Right after he leaves, it starts to rain—not seriously, just an intermittent drizzle here and there, as if testing the equipment for later. The men depart, leaving wrappers and beer cans in their wake. A blond woman walks up to the fountain, the most delicious little caramel boy toddling after her. It's amazing how many interracial couples there are in Paris. In two days, I've seen more beige children than I did in a year in Manhattan. The night before, Frankie told me how much he misses Italy, but said this would be the perfect city in which to raise our own 2.5. True, being a nanny was like living in Hell with weekends off, but I've always looked forward to the day when I can get some self-control, be able to stop chain smoking and chain drinking, and have a kid of my own.

I watch the lady chase her baby around the fountain, the way she pretends he's running too fast for her, then suddenly makes a grab for him. He shrieks with delight as he dodges her each time.

The next thing I know, I'm the only one in the park. I look at my watch. Frankie has been gone for half an hour.

He isn't coming back. He isn't coming back and I have 53¢ and no idea how to get the hell out of St. Denis. How could I do this to myself? What an idiot . . . what a maroon. Here's this great-looking guy who's half in love with me. He's provided sleep, food, three orgasms. I've been a bitch—just because he doesn't fit in with the Ralph Lauren ads that wallpaper my brain.

It's the worst thing that could happen to me, and it's all my fault. It won't be the first time I've pushed someone away who was trying to help. I hate my place in the world; that much is certain. I just wish I knew why it always makes me chase away the people who try to save me from it.

Close to an hour later, when I am writing incoherent and unpunctuated thoughts in my journal, Frankie plops down next to me.

"*Dio,* he wasn't home either! So I went to his job, where they told me . . . what?"

I turn away so he can't see the tears that have gathered in my eyes. "You said five, ten minutes," I say through clenched teeth. "I've been sitting here in the rain for nearly an hour. I'd thought you'd left me. I thought you'd left me in this horrible . . . " The tears fall and I wipe them away angrily, waiting for his arm to come around me. It doesn't come. When I glance at him, he's as wooden as the bench, glaring at the trickle of a fountain in front of us.

We sit in silence for a minute, but I feel better. He came back. He really does care. He isn't going to leave me all alone. And what must he be going through right now? If he didn't have help from his family before, when it was just him, then obviously help isn't easy to get.

"I'm sorry. I don't know what's gotten into me today. I know you're doing a lot for us." I lay my head on his shoulder. Half a beat, then his arm comes up and around me. Out of the corner of my eye, I see him nod a little bit, like I'd come this close to pissing him off for good. I hate him.

The Métro station is just a few feet away, a giant overpass with a pedestrian mall inside.

"You got my phone number, right?" he asks. I nod and pat the piece of paper I've slipped into my knapsack. It's right next to the calling card I got in Italy.

"But why can't I wait with you?" I'm careful to keep my voice non-confrontational.

"Because I'm going to a construction site to find my cousin—no place for a girl. Like I said, we'll meet at the Eiffel Tower at eight, same place we met last night. Nine o'clock at the latest."

Seven hours is a lot of time to kill. But tonight I'm going to have a place to sleep, a job, someone to hold on to.

Best of all, I'm going back to Paris.

Frankie hands me a Métro ticket, kisses me on the forehead. "Be safe." He starts to walk away.

Suddenly he comes back, kisses me on the mouth. "*Ciao, bella.*"

THE FIRST TIME everyone sees the Champs-Elysées, it should be a mild evening, light rain, denim sky. I float through the crowds, popping in and out of the malls, waiting out a heavy downpour with a crowd under the awning at Virgin Records, another under an office building with a guy named Roman, from Romania. He shares his grapes with me. "Paris is full of strangers," he tells me in English. "It's hard, but you can make it."

When the rain stops, the air grows warmer and the sweet smell of moist earth mixes with that of the newly fallen leaves. I trace my way along the Seine, making mental notes of the cafés Frankie and I will patronize once we get settled. I don't get lost at all and make it to the Eiffel Tower just before eight.

The rain has rendered the field across the street a bog. It's started to drizzle again, so I stand underneath an awning by a ticket window. A group of middle-aged American couples banter a few feet away.

"There are no bathrooms in this country."

"And the ones there are, you have to pay."

"It's just forty cents!"

"In Florida, the bathrooms are free."

"Which is why no one can ever stand to use them. Dave, where in tarnation are you going?" One of the men has broken rank, is heading across the pavement underneath the base of the tower.

"Said he thinks he knows where a bathroom is, spotted one by the carousel."

"He's going to get wet for nothing. Then he'll wake up tomorrow too sick to do anything. Just like our honeymoon."

"Where'd y'all honeymoon?"

"Disneyland." Appreciative whoops of laughter. This is a mixed group: Southerners, Midwesterners.

Could I go back to America with you guys? I want to ask them. *I'm supposed to go home with someone else. Only he doesn't have a home. And I don't even know him.*

NINE FIFTEEN PM. This time, I'm not even going to sweat it. I move back across the street, to the sidewalk just outside the park. I realize I don't even know how Frankie will be coming. In a car driven by one of his friends, I hope. I watch as each one comes slowly up the street, then passes me. It starts to rain harder, this time bringing a deep chill to the air.

Nine forty-nine PM. Maybe I'm waiting in the wrong place. He could be here, searching for me, and the big tour bus parked in front of me is blocking his view. I walk up and down the puddly street, back underneath the tower, my head oscillating like a fan. The military guards toting M16s up and down the perimeter have begun to recognize me. I stamp a scowl on my face. Better to be thought a terrorist than to be stood up. There I go, overreacting again. I already know my boy has no sense of time. I head back to my post.

"Excuse me, do you know if it's okay to park here?" Another American, a sleek brunette, stepping out of a red sports car.

"Oh, sure, people have been doing it all night." I'm clenching my teeth to keep the shiver out of my voice.

"Come on, Chelsea hon." A teenage version of the woman climbs out from the passenger side, her head craned upward. Mother and daughter wear matching leather coats, the kind with fur inside. Chelsea's door, which her mother has to remind her to close, emits a scent of cherry air freshener, warmth. The girl doesn't take her eyes off the tower as her mother links her arm through hers. "First time," the woman mouths in my direction. She leads her daughter toward the lights.

Eleven fifteen PM. I'm hiding behind a tree a little ways into the park so no one will see me: the mother and daughter, the guards, the tour buses that come and go every forty minutes. I begin to think maybe Frankie isn't coming.

Shivering so badly I can barely walk, I make my way to a phone booth, only to find my Italian calling card is not accepted in snobby French pay phones.

Raindrops crash and die against the glass of the booth. I'm penniless, abandoned by a man in Paris, like a character from a Jean Rhys novel.

I think of a line from one of her books: "the shriek of Paris." I press my head against the glass of the phone booth, hearing it for the first time.

FOUR THINGS I LEARNED FROM BEING HOMELESS IN PARIS

1) PARIS IS NO PLACE TO BE HOMELESS.

Even the bathrooms cost money. When I do get to pee, it feels wrong, as though I'm wetting the bed and can't stop. Like I did when I was little and my mother wouldn't talk to me the entire morning: *Sesame Street* and peanut butter sandwiches served in a black cloud of silence.

2) WHATEVER YOU DO, DON'T SMILE.

I think I'll go mad from my lips' being chapped. Within two days, a stiff protective skin forms over them, but if I drink water or lick them, I'm in agony again. I watch lustfully as people apply soothing pink Chapstick, shiny tubs of balm. Even worse are the preteen girls with their constant application of flavored gel: banana, strawberry shortcake . . . why, you could make a meal of it! I want to grab one from some shiny-lipped torturer and run screaming into the night.

3) TAKE TIME TO REFLECT AT THE END OF EACH DAY.
I am lucky to discover the bathrooms at the famed museum-library Centre Pompidou. First of all, they're free. The grey metallic walls and doors stretch from ceiling to floor, giving visitors complete privacy. There's usually not a line, and I debate curling up on the floor and taking a catnap. What I do is take off my socks and check the progress of my feet. My socks are either wet or stiff from being wet previously. They make a dry, scraping sound as I pull them off. The soles of my feet are a succession of grimacing splits, as though they've been whipped. These have lines of black through them—clots of string from the socks. The red polish on my toes has turned into tiny island nations.

There's a lot of noise in the bathroom: flushing and hand washing and dryers and chatter. This leaves me free to lay my head against the wall and dry-scream, which is sort of like whispering at the top of your lungs. I learned to do this into a pillow at home after a spanking, when crying for more than a minute meant I wanted more. Now I do it right before closing, before I have to walk out into All Night Long. *I can't go back out there. Please don't make me, please.* The fluorescent light overhead flickers and squeaks as though any minute it will short out.

4) PARISIANS ARE SO NOT UNFRIENDLY.

There are men who walk slowly through the night streets. They know that the bus at the stop where I'm huddled doesn't run on Mondays, that nobody with any hope stares at a river for that long.

"*Bonsoir.* Cold out tonight, isn't it? Would you like to go with me for a drink?...*Mais oui,* you are right, all the bars are closed now, but I do have a bottle at home, you know....*Oh là là,* your hands are like the ice....I'm sorry, you don't like to be touched, but that is how we do in France....You are very pretty, you know....Will you come with me? Can I go with you? You are walking awfully fast. Do you know where you are going? It is not a good night to be lost!"

ALONE

CH. 06

I wander back down the Seine and up the steps of the Musée de la Sculpture en Plein Air, a collection of writhing metal that claws toward the sky like a forest of burnt trees. Past it are steps that lead down to the river. I settle on one behind some bushes. It's close to the street, in case anyone tries to attack me, private enough that I can let go and shiver to my heart's content. It's like finally getting to scratch that mosquito bite on your ass.

I smell the pot before I hear the voices. Three young guys come from behind a nook nearby, glancing at me as they pass. I clench to keep from shaking, but when they greet me, my own "*bonsoir*" trembles in return.

One of them comes back. Pop-star hair, slick clothes. He's cute, except for his face. He looks like the type who laughs at his own jokes before he finishes them.

"*Ça va?*" he asks. Everything okay?

"*Ça va.*" I convulse.

"You are cold," he observes, sitting next to me. We exchange names. His is Brian. He asks what I'm doing out here this time of night; what is it, 2:00 AM? I don't have enough French to be evasive. This leaves me with shrugging. The river laps against a big white tourist barge, at rest for the night.

He sits closer. Puts his arm around my shoulder. God forgive me, but he is warm; I let him.

Don't I have anywhere to go? I shake my head, staring glumly in front of me. But I'm checking him out: keys to a sports car on his lap, new white sneakers, heavy gold chain worn over his shirt. This is the kind of guy who makes money to spend it.

From the sidewalk, his friends call. They're wearing expensive tracksuits like his, look like his backup singers. They peek over the bushes at us, giggling. Brian says something harsh to them and they duck out of sight.

"You are very pretty, you know that?"

"Thanks." As an afterthought, I smile. Rain and tears have made such an agony of my chapped lips, I almost scream. I bite the lower one to stifle the scream. This doesn't help.

God only knows what this guy thinks of me. My hair and jeans are soaked. My voice sounds flat even to my own ears. Even if my smile made me seem like a normal person, I'm sure I ruined it with the Munch-esque look of agony right after. And all the while, I'm shaking so hard with cold, I must look like a blur. One thing's for certain:

Brian is no mind reader, because if he knew what I was thinking, he'd be out of here in a shot.

Until I was in my early twenties, I honestly believed that all people wanted to kill themselves at least some of the time, and that they were just better at hiding it than I was. I was disabused of this notion by several friends, a few therapists, and one ashen-faced bartender. So I learned to keep my thoughts of escape—the not *if* but *when*—to myself; else I would have turned to this guy and explained my dilemma.

Should I stay or should I go? Was meeting Frankie the night before like being given a chance to start over? Or was losing him a sign that it was all too late, that I'd been meant to die and my cowardice would only lead to more heartbreak?

Not to mention there's a looming third option, more terrifying because I haven't considered it, and it just might be beyond my control.

Before I met Frankie, starvation seemed like a quick, unpainful way out. Not to mention the added benefit of letting my friends see that the binge-drinking, chain-smoking, mood-swinging girl they all teased for her lack of self-control had more of it than all of them put together. ("A hunger artist," they'd whisper, awestruck, throwing flowers on my skinny coffin.)

But now I'm beginning to think it won't be easy at all. In the last three days, I've eaten twice. During that time, I've spent at least double the amount of hours walking as I have asleep. There's an abyss in my gut and a roaring emptiness in my head. The rush of cars on the rain-soaked streets is starting to sound like tidal waves. An hour before, Notre Dame, bathed in the darkness, heaved a shuddering sigh as I walked past, as though impatient with me for still being alive. My fear of my growing weakness is making me weaker still. Just because I can't afford a hotel room or a meal doesn't mean I can afford to walk the streets all night like this.

"Think, think," I hiss to myself, pretending to study the boats, feeling this guy Brian's eyes on me. I know he's got something to do with my next step. I can barely understand the half phrases and pictures my mind is flashing at me, but after a bit of effort, a theme begins to unify them.

Sleep . . . you need some . . . somewhere warm and dry . . . mind even more than body. . . . If your mind leaves you first, your mind will leave you trapped. . . .

I get an idea: I'm going to get this guy to drive me around in his car for eight hours so I can get some sleep. All I have to do is figure out how to say in French, "Pardon me, but it appears I've changed my mind about dying."

"*Très jolie.*" I catch his hand midway up my thigh.

"What are you doing?"

"Give me a kiss. Just a little one." He puckers his lips. They're shiny. I swear I catch a hint of some fruity smell, melon maybe. He has some kind of gloss on! Even as I shrink back, I half consider grabbing his face, smearing my lips against his.

"C'mon . . . " He's whispering my name in my ear. I'm beginning to be sorry I told him what it was. I push his hand away again. "Why would I want to kiss you?"

"Because you are so pretty."

"No, that's why you want to kiss me." From behind the bushes, his friends burst out laughing. Brian jumps up. Hisses exchange. The boys' snickering drifts away.

"*Bon,* now we are alone." He sits back down, rolling up his sleeves. "Now will you kiss me?"

"No, I'm not like that," I tell him. *Especially,* I think, *when you have a chin as big as my foot.* I'm shaking uncontrollably again, and he rubs my shoulders.

What's wrong with you? my mind screams, over the sound of my chattering teeth. Not only am I struggling, against the face of all rationality, to survive, but some ill-timed sense of pride is thwarting what might be my only chance to do so. Why I don't just fool around with this guy so I can sleep in his bed for a few hours? Do I still want to die? Is that it? And if so, why am I so determined to protect this body I want so badly to escape from?

It occurs to me that something is seriously wrong with my mind, and I can't just call it sleep. I seem to have this fissure that enables me to be both victim and tyrant. To want desperately to escape my life while doing anything I can to survive.

Brian's phone rings, to the tune of Biggie Smalls' "Fucking You Tonight."

Well, almost anything.

"No." His voice is grim when he answers. "Not yet."

"Listen," he says briskly, hanging up. "Are you going to kiss me or what?"

How do you say, "Help me?" in French? How do you say it in English?

"*D'accord.* My friends are headed back to the house; they want to drink." He stands. "I'm going."

I curl and uncurl my stiff fingers. "*Ciao.*" He remains standing over me for a moment; I flinch when he kneels back down, this time offering his cheek.

"One little kiss, right here."

I lift my knees, bury my head in my arms. With my eyes closed, I try to visualize the world I would want if I could have anything. All I see is blackness. When I look up, I'm alone.

Just before dawn, as I trudge up and down along the Seine, I figure it out. *Don't fight the cold. No shivering or hunching or rubbing your hands. Just let it have its way with you. Let it do what it wants. That won't make it go away. You still feel the cold; you just no longer feel yourself.*

I DIDN'T LEARN to walk until I was ten. I skipped everywhere. Everywhere except for the places I ran. As I skipped, I would leap so high into the air that for a moment my feet would wiggle uselessly, like Fred Flintstone's. I sang whatever popped into my head: Christmas carols, Top 40 hits, the entire soundtrack to *Annie,* everything at the top of my lungs.

"What's for dinner?" I'd ask each night. No matter what the answer—meat loaf, tuna casserole, Shake 'n Bake chicken and tater tots—it would send me into paroxysms of joy. When watching TV, I'd get so excited for my programs to come on that I'd dance to the theme songs. My favorite show was *Batman and Robin.* During the Dynamic Duo's fight scenes, I'd hop on the couch, punching and kicking the air in assistance. My exuberant nature extended to my social life. Every kid I met became my instant friend. I struck up conversations with strangers like I was running for office.

Because of this joie de vivre (for which, these days, I surely would be medicated), the head teacher at the small private school I attended grew fond of me. When I was seven, Mrs. Whidby invited me to travel to Connecticut with her, her husband, and their brood of adopted kids. Friends of theirs lived in the country, at the end of a car-free road bordered by woods. It was my first time away from my home in bullet-ridden Newark, New Jersey, where we'd moved when I was still a baby. I couldn't believe I was allowed to go outside without an adult. Long after the other kids had gone in to watch TV, I would be riding a bike, running through the fields, or just lying on my back, staring at the sky through the high grass. When it got too dark to see, I'd sit on the porch, listening to the various sounds a country summer allows. The woods would grow a shade of black I thought happened only in fairytales. Staring at it for too long made me nervous, as though a monster lurked within—something that had been waiting its whole life just for me.

One night, as I sat on the hamper and watched Mrs. Whidby bathe her two youngest sons, I asked, "How long have we been here?" When she told me, I announced, "Well, that means I haven't cried in five whole days!"

"Why would you cry?" Mrs. Whidby asked absentmindedly, shampooing a curly head. "Aren't you having fun?"

"Yeah, but usually I cry every day."

My teacher looked up at me slowly. "What did you say?"

Fear slipped cold from my chest to my toes. Now, I'd done it. I was a happy, easygoing kid at school. I never so much as pouted (unless snacktime was late). So when did I cry? And why?

As Mrs. Whidby studied me, I realized my hand had gone to my mouth. She couldn't find out the truth!

To look at me, you would never think I was anything but a nice little girl. At home, my nickname was Mocha, just like the color of my skin. I had chubby cheeks and wore my hair in four chubby braids (actually, at that age, I had chubby everything). My brown eyes were so wide, they bordered on anime.

But the fact remained that I was really a fucking little pain-in-the-ass bitch. If Mrs. Whidby found out, I'd never get to be line leader again. She'd tell the other teachers, who'd tell all the other kids, and the whole world would know how bad I was. How every day, within two hours of coming home, I'd cause my mother to become so mad that she made sure I, in turn, ended up sobbing, my face buried in the swamp my pillow had become.

"April Fools'!" I said. Considering it was midsummer, this was ridiculous, even for a seven-year-old. Mrs. Whidby was about to say something, when the bigger boy dunked the smaller one's head into the tub. Amid the subsequent wailing and scolding, I was able to slip out into the night. I stood on the porch, facing the black woods. They buzzed with crickets, which managed to sound both frightening and terrified at the same time.

THE LAST THING I want to be is a one-hit wonder: a person who's beaten the odds and fled their abusive family, then sat down in the middle of their life. I know a score of them: gay men who fled their hick towns; artistic souls who dropped out of med school; a Hindu girl who fled the night before her arranged marriage. I once had a roommate whose mother used to beat her and her siblings when she didn't win the Powerball; my roommate was the only one of the seven kids who had moved out. It's a triumph, of course, that people like this survive, until you see that surviving is all they can do. They work menial jobs and sleep on people's couches and sleep with everyone and start crying after their third drink and stop crying after their seventh and they freeze. It's like after turning off the road that was laid before them; they've never been able to find their way home.

THE NEXT AFTERNOON, refreshed by a nap in the Bois de Boulogne, I head back to the river. It's been over twenty-four hours since I've last eaten, and my head feels so light I have to keep holding on to the sides of buildings to steady myself. As I walk, I wonder if maybe Frankie didn't mean to stand me up. Maybe he's looking for me now. Maybe I don't have to do this. If only I could call him. I take to glancing into phone booths to see if anyone's left a card with some minutes on it. In the third one, there's a sandwich.

A sandwich. I enter the booth, closing the door behind me. The sound of my breathing fills the narrow space. The sandwich, set on top of the phone, is wrapped in foil, the bitten tip sticking out. I look all about me. Two waiters are chatting by the tables in an empty café. In the shop next door, a clerk is showing a woman a lamp. Behind me, traffic whizzes by. I grab the sandwich and run . . . smack into the glass. I've forgotten to open the door.

I slip on my sunglasses and try again, bearing my prize past the curious gaze of half the block.

With that sandwich (once I'm around the corner), I become a normal person. I'm a student, an office worker, feeling a little munchy after a productive day, so I stopped to buy a snack. No time to linger in a café; I have someone waiting for me: my family, a lover, a rowdy group of girlfriends who get together every Tuesday for wine and a three-hanky film.

I sit on a nearby bench to inspect the sub. Layered inside a baguette are lettuce and tomato, ham, mashed egg yolk mixed with some kind of orange flavoring, the whites sliced underneath. I pull off the nibbled part of the sandwich. Even with that, it can't be more than three bites old.

The first swallow burns like acid. My throat is bone dry. I remove from my bag and drink the entire bottle of water I've been depriving myself of, the faster to starve to death. My thirst sated, the sandwich becomes one of the best things I've ever eaten: big, lush, filling. I dine at a small park, watching traffic careen around the Arc de Triomphe. There are other people on the benches: chatting on phones, watching the sun go down. Just some folks taking a moment at the end of the day; I am one of them.

BEING HOMELESS IS boring. Once you've managed to satisfy all bodily needs, snagged yourself a cigarette, and realized the weather's not trying to kill you, there's nothing to do. You're too tired to enjoy the park. Words swim and blur on a page. What's playing at the movies? Oh, never mind.

You do two things.

You watch. You watch the grand parade of life pass you by. Trench coats and shiny shoes racing for the train. Children on their way to school, knapsacks bouncing as they walk. Lovers in cafés and skateboarders in the Bastille and shop workers staring out the window. Cell phones and shopping bags and steaming paper cups—people have these things and don't seem to consider it a miracle.

When you can't look anymore because it's all there just to hurt you, you think back. Sleeping late on a rainy morning, padding across the kitchen in your slippers to make tea, the smell of a book you've just bought. Sometimes you think of your friends and wonder what the heck it was you talked about that was so funny. You used to wait in line at the bank, and when it was your turn, they gave you money. You were always late: for work, dinner, dates. Were constantly racing through the city streets, thinking of an excuse. You'd go from one place to another, and you belonged in both of them. You used to look in the refrigerator for something to eat and lean your head against the wall as you played back your messages. You'd get foot rubs and give foot rubs. A boyfriend saying, "I love these hips" before he kissed them. The smooth look of peanut butter when you first open the jar. Any stray memory. Anywhere but here.

THE
AFRICAN'S
QUEEN

CH. 07

ejuvenated after my first meal all day, I wander around until I come across the Pont des Arts. The wooden bridge reminds me of the boardwalk along the Jersey shore. It's the first time I've come across it, and I can't bring myself to leave. The night is growing cool, but I still feel rosy from the sandwich. Couples stroll along; packs of skateboarders do tricks off the benches. I want to talk to someone, anyone. *Hasn't the weather been crazy lately? Any bookstores open this late? You know, I've been here four days and I can't get over how beautiful this place is. Cute dog.*

A tall guy in a red shirt sits down next to me, leaning forward to watch a dinner boat full of tourists tug by. He says something in French, too low for me to hear.

"*Pardon?*" I ask.

"Oh, nothing," he answers, not looking at me. "I was just talking to myself."

Right. My cue to find another bench. Instead, I lean forward as well and we both stare at the boat until it's out of sight.

"You are *americaine?*"

"You're talking to me now?"

The guy laughs, drumming on his knees. He's not from here, either. He's from Senegal. Have I heard of it? (People who come from small countries are always anxious to know if you've heard of them.) Am I here on vacation, a student? I shrug. I don't want to think of anything bad, like my life. I had a sandwich today; let's talk about that.

He's wearing some sort of red uniform shirt over a thermal top. "Do you work on one of these boats?" I ask. He never stops staring after them, will barely look at me.

He shakes his head and offers a rambling explanation of which I understand not a word. My French, what I can remember from school, is halting but textbook perfect. He is fluent but his French is bad, his accent strange. I ask him to speak more slowly. This causes him to wave his hands faster as he speaks. I give up.

"Do you have a cigarette?"

No, but he'll get one from his friends. Before I can stop him, he's dashed down the bridge and back again, coming back with a lit Marlboro from one of the skateboarders. He eyes it steadily as I smoke. I pretend not to notice. Under the circumstances, I can hardly be expected to share.

Do I have a boyfriend?

Not right now.

He sits up straight and begins drumming on his knees, the bench, his feet tapping a bass line. People walking by stare.

"Why are you doing that?"

"I don't have a girlfriend, either. Know why?" *Thump-tap-thump.* "The girls in Paris, *elles sont bizarres.* They want a man with money, his own car."

I laugh, giddy from the cigarette. "That's all the girls in the world," I say. The boy drops his head and stops drumming. A boat chugs by; he fastens his eyes upon it.

"What's your name?" I ask quickly.

He whips out his passport. It's dated from last year, but the boy in the picture looks a decade younger. "What kind of name is Otenaba Luciano Hatumba?"

"My mother." He shrugs. "She was crazy."

"Mine too," I say. He tells me I can call him anything I want.

SOMETIMES, JUST AS we were drifting off to sleep, my mother would call to us, "Bay-bees? Where are my cheeldrens? They are sleeping, yes? Bay-bees, eef you are awake, koom to mee!" Stewie and I would sit up in our twin beds, our grins flashing in the dark. Euro-Mommy had arrived!

We would kick up a tsunami of blankets and pad down the hall on our pajama-d feet. In the living room, the TV would be on, usually featuring whatever program had generated the accent in the first place. My father's eyes would be fixed on us, half-threatening us, half-pleading with us not to ask my mother why she was speaking like

Sophia Loren in *Houseboat*, Charo on *The Love Boat*, or Zsa Zsa Gabor in … well, anything. Euro-Mommy was totally deeferent from the one we were trapped with inside the apartment every day. Rather than rejoicing when we finally went to bed, she missed her bay-bees. She rolled her *r*'s in such a hilarious way, I almost choked on the wine she let me drink from her glass.

"In my country, they let the cheeldren have a beet of the wine, no?" she would say to my father when he protested. He didn't too arduously, however. Euro-Mommy never yelled and cursed at him, only made expansive hand gestures as she waxed philosophical over such questions as "Why you no make zee money like zee real man?"

None of this seemed the least bit unusual until I was eight. I had just been allowed to go to sleepovers, where I noticed something strange: During the impromptu pillow fights and ghost stories told by flashlight, my friends' mothers would yell up to us to go to sleep, or else. But no matter how late at night it was, or what they had been watching, the other mothers retained their nationality.

At six, Stewie took Euro-Mommy as a matter of course. He ran up to her and curled up on her lap, happy that she was happy. I followed my father into the kitchen, where he always made coffee for the inevitable Julio Gallo hangover.

"Dad, why does she always talk like that?" I whispered. He had opened the Chock Full o'Nuts and was just staring into it.

"Accents, they can happen to anyone." Usually I loved my dad's puns. When I didn't laugh at this one, he added, "Mommy's special. She's got a lot of people living inside her."

"None of 'em are going to turn into another little brother, are they?"

"I'm talking about people from her other lives. Remember we talked about reincarnation?" I nodded. "Well, sometimes people have the souls of who they used to be inside them. Especially," he added, "if they're not happy."

I looked down at my feet. Despite my footy pajamas, they were cold against the kitchen floor. From the living room, I could hear my mother singing "Frère Jacques" to Stewie. My father had refilled her wineglass and handed it to me.

"Where's my wine?" I whined.

"I'm not even going to answer that." He turned to put the jug of red back in the fridge.

"Aw, come on! Come on, Dad!" With my free hand, I pounded the small of his back. "I've earned this."

He whirled around so fast that half the wine in the glass I was holding leapt onto the ground. Whatever my father was about to say was forgotten as he grabbed a roll of Bounty and fell to his knees. My mother hated a sticky floor.

"You haven't earned anything." His head was down as he wiped the stain. "You don't know the meaning of the word."

LUCIANO, THE SENEGALESE guy, doesn't work anywhere, doesn't live anywhere. (For some reason, I find this incredible.) He's been here eight months. Paris is very hard. Where he comes from, no one has anything. It's like God has forgotten all about them. But here, where people have so much and he still has nothing, it's like God is laughing at him. He bums cigarettes for me as we walk, runs up to people who aren't even smoking to ask. I limp ahead as far as I can, my face burning with embarrassment. The only time I slow down is when he actually gets me one.

THERE WERE CERTAIN things you couldn't do. You couldn't say, "Hey, man," or talk too loudly or use pepper or eat what my mother called "nigger foods": chili, Fig Newtons, bologna sandwiches with no cheese. You couldn't watch *Good Times* or *Sanford and Son* or *What's Happening!!* (*Fat Albert* was allowed, because it was animated.) Packets of Kool-Aid, I had to smuggle under my coat like gin.

There were niggers and there were Nice Black People, my mother would say. Her voice changed when she spoke of the latter; it became like the voice she switched to upon answering the phone after screaming at my father. Niggers came in all shapes and sizes but were easily recognizable. They were always pointed out to us from the car window. Nice Black People were few and far between: Bill Cosby, the woman who did the six o'clock news. And, my mother assured us, she wasn't the only one doing the pointing. White people (who seemed to all be nice, unless they rode motorcycles) would also be watching, trying to determine which kind we were. My brother and I, well behaved and quiet to the point of elective muteness, would gaze wistfully at children of all races as they made their parents chase them through the mall, screamed for candy in the supermarket, hurled themselves onto the floor, overcome with the grief of the small.

We were driven miles to private schools my mother approved of, kept in the house when we lived in neighborhoods she did not. The latter left time for a lot of covert reading: Maya Angelou, Toni Morrison. I spent the year I was thirteen poring over what I originally thought was "The Autobiography of Malcolm the Tenth." High school was my first truly integrated experience. After the Rodney King riots, the black kids decided to do a walkout against the establishment. It was held after seventh period so no one would miss lunch. When the bell rang, they all poured out of the classrooms and onto the front lawn. Some were chanting. Homemade signs bobbed above the crowd. All the other kids ran to the windows to watch, giddy with the ensuing disorder. There was a girls' bathroom on the third floor that no one ever used; the toilets didn't flush. I hid there for what felt like hours, until all the shouting had stopped.

BLUE BLOOD IS THICKER THAN WATER

CH. 08

hâtelet les Halles will come to remind me of Greenwich Village: ethnic eateries, thrift shops, sidewalk vendors, students and tourists all vying for space along the twisting streets. But when Luciano first takes me there, at ten o'clock that night, it seems to me some medieval minstrel show. Along the glass-topped mall we weave through crowds gathered before singers, jugglers, breakdancers. Two mimes follow us a couple of paces, until I jab a lit cigarette at them. Kids with tattoos, piercings, and crayon-colored hair swig bottles of wine and grope each other against the old stone walls. Boom boxes blare beside groups of friends stretched out on the sidewalk as comfortably as if they were in a basement den. Luciano introduces me to a couple holding court atop a heating grate. They are cloaked in blankets, eating something out of a pizza box. It isn't pizza.

"Oh, America!" The girl claps. Her hands are as pudgy as her cheeks. She is missing her front teeth. "I love America."

"Have you ever been?"

"Oh, noo…." Her boyfriend stands up, clutching his blanket about him like a cape, and kisses my hand. He welcomes me to Paris. I am in good hands, he assures me. Luciano will take care of me.

On cue, my escort asks me if I'm hungry. He dashes under the metal grates of a shop about to close and comes out with a round loaf of bread and some cheese.

"Did you … did you just … ?" I pantomime "steal."

No, no, don't be silly, he laughs. He just went in and asked the owner if we could have some food, as we have nothing to eat. On second thought, he has a better idea. He instructs me to put the food in my knapsack, which I struggle to do as he drags me over to a panini shop. The young cooks obviously know him. They smile at me appraisingly while Luciano explains how hungry I am.

Aha! Dying of embarrassment! Why haven't I thought of that?

The panino, filled with some kind of soft meat, is delicious, so hot it's smoking. Soon I feel warm and sleepy. The shop lights and jangly music lose their appeal. Luciano leads me to a bus stop—a nice one, the traffic side obscured by a tree, enabling people to huddle in near privacy. I stand up to check the name of the stop so I can come back to it. When I sit back down, Luciano's arm goes around my shoulder.

Have I mentioned that he's cute? No? That's because he's not.

I clear my throat. Um, listen. I'm not looking for anything, nothing more serious than a friend.

Luciano stares at the ground for a minute, then nods. He wears a rather determined expression, as though calculating just how many potted meat sandwiches and filched cigarettes he's going to have to feed me before he wins my heart.

He begins to drum again, scraping his feet on the sidewalk and pounding on the glass. My head begins to feel heavy, like a balloon filled with sand. Isn't he tired?

Of course, *rap rap pound,* he's always tired, *boom rap boom,* but not to worry—he'll spend the night up with me. Do I think the sun is going to come out tomorrow? He knows a good place to watch it rise.

Listen—he has to find me a bed. He has to sleep. Somewhere, sometime. He tells me about the shelters they have on the outskirts of town. I'll get a bed, breakfast in the morning. Of course, we'll have to be separated.

"No," I say.

"Why not? There's one just—"

"No, no, no. Don't you have any friends nearby?"

He has one who lives not too far from here. But the friend likes women. If Luciano takes me there, we'd have to . . .

"We have a saying in France," he mumbles, "'ménage à trois.' It means . . ."

We have it, too. Never mind.

I start looking around, plotting my escape. What am I doing with this guy? He has no place to stay, no cigarettes. He probably doesn't even have 53¢, like I do. And he can't seem to go for five seconds without pounding a staccato on the nearest surface. If I'm going to be destitute and pathetic, I can do it by myself.

Luciano seems to read my mind, because suddenly he jumps up, blocking my path. Wait a minute, he *does* know some people. They stay on the other side of the river. He's sure they won't mind if I stay the night with them.

No group sex?

Pas du tout.

Oh, thank you, God. Thankyouthankyouthankyou. I grab Luciano's arm and give it a squeeze. He looks so pleased, I amend it by adding a sisterly pat.

First I'll take a shower. No, first I'll pee. With the sudden onslaught of all that food and water, I feel like I've swallowed an aquarium. After that, I'll take a shower, a long, hot one. If the tub is clean, I'll lie on my back and hold my poor feet up to the spray. Then to bed. Maybe it will be a couch, some blankets on the floor. No matter. *Oh, to stretch out indoors, to be warm. . . . Oh, look, we're crossing the river. The Left Bank! . . . Oh, to be warm in a fashionable neighborhood. . . . Oh, we're going down the steps leading to the river. . . . Oh?*

"These friends of yours, they live on a houseboat?" I ask, lightly, desperately.

His friends, the ones he bummed the first cigarette from, are squatters. They sleep on a ledge in a hollow of the wall facing the river. Their shelter takes up half the space. Luciano is always welcome to the other half. Barring the weekends, of course, when they entertain.

"Are you crazy?" I hiss. "You expect me to sleep in a hole in the wall?" (Boy, that French is coming back now.)

Shh. He points to the half of the wall covered in boxes, blue tarp over the top. If you listen carefully, you can hear the snores.

I watch as he hops onto the empty half of the ledge, reaching into the lean-to and pulling out a sponge the size of a full mattress. When he takes out the sheets, I climb up to help him arrange them over the ledge. There are holes torn in the sheets to match up with the bolts in the stone walls, so that they can be fastened to make a sort of tent. I lift up the mattress as directed, so he can tuck the sheets underneath. Our weight, he explains, will keep the sheet from flying up. It'll be just like a door.

There's a big blue blanket that smells of dirty diapers and room freshener. We wrap ourselves up in it. I take off my sweater so I won't have to put my face against the giant sponge. Do we say goodnight? The sheet billows in the wind like the belly of a fat, laughing ghost. I turn my back to the wall. I still have to pee. I am aware of every second I sleep, of pulling the covers up to my face, then remembering where I am and snatching them away.

"It's not so bad, I guess." I forget and whisper this in English, maybe because the person I'm trying to convince is me. "We can pretend we're in a dungeon. In a castle."

"*Il fait froid. Il fait froid.*" Luciano shudders. Then I hear only the wind.

THE NIGHT I learned I was fallen royalty did not start well. My parents, brother, and I had just dropped my great-grandmother off after dinner and were headed home. The silence in the car, interrupted by an occasional burp-masquerading-as-hiccup, had been induced by a satiety possible only after Wednesday night's all-you-can-eat surf 'n' turf at Bob's Big Boy.

Yet I was in a sour mood. I'd had to miss playing at a friend's house for the biannual and obligatory dinner with an old bore named Nana, like a taunt. My great-grandmother was a small, yellow woman with tight salt-and-pepper curls and a face like a bulldog's. She never missed a chance to press a nickel or half-unwrapped lemon drop into the hands of her "grandbabies" and then demand a kiss. Her beringed fingers always pointed to exactly the spot on her cheek where the little hairs were sharpest. Certainly, she knew how to enjoy being taken out to dinner. Without fail, she would order the most expensive thing on the menu, even if she had to ask the waiter what was in it. She talked incessantly throughout the meal, food particles flying from her mouth like partially masticated acrobats. Before appetizers were over, Stewie had to put his napkin over his face for protection. I was too big to get away with that, but as I picked a piece of french fry from my hair, I said, "Nana's gross! I wish she wasn't related to us."

Silence greeted this remark, a common occurrence when I made the mistake of being honest. I could've rectified the situation by quickly borrowing a line from the *Big Book of Don't Hit Me*—something like "Just kidding!" or "My tummy hurts!" or "I love you, Mommy." But before I could think of anything, my mother turned around and smiled.

"She's not, you know. Grandma was adopted."

"She was?" I leaned up toward the front seat. My mother glanced at my father, as though to gauge whether we were old enough to know the truth. Angled toward my mother, I couldn't see him at all. The car heater blew hot air into my face.

"I think you guys are finally old enough now to hear the family secret." The secret! The reason Mommy was always telling us we were the most specialest people in the world. We were finally going to learn why! My mother studied both of us in turn. I sat up straight and stiff as a board, unable to breathe. Stewie yanked his finger out of his nose, clasping his hands on his lap as tightly as mine.

"Do you promise not to tell anyone the secret of our family?" We nodded. "Not even other family?"

At this, Stewie and I exchanged a look. Since he could talk, I'd been telling him he was from outer space, but my God, what if we all were?

"No need to look like that," my mother chuckled. "It's a good thing. Actually, it's wonderful."

ONCE UPON A time, at the end of World War I, there was a soldier who didn't want to go home. He had grown up in a poor, black hamlet in the South, where the blood of the KKK's victims often mixed with the red Georgia roads. He had been stationed in the French countryside, and after liberation, the grateful village threw open its arms to fete the stationed troops. There were parties and speeches and long nights in pubs, where men, black and white, sat together, laughing at the attempts to speak each other's language. The villagers did not look at the soldier as a servant or a beast. He was an American, a hero, a man.

The night before they were to ship home, there was a formal sendoff at the village's grandest estate. In this mansion the soldier saw things he hadn't thought possible: silver bowls, white servants, and a French girl, the host's daughter, who kept meeting his eyes across the ballroom floor.

The French girl was as beautiful as the soldier was handsome, and as restless. Her parents were *vicomtes* for whom propriety and tradition still formed the parameters of life. Their daughter's betrothal to a man fifteen years her senior was to be fulfilled the next year, when she completed finishing school.

The other soldiers wanted to talk to the young lady of the house. She, however, preferred to chat with the soldier who sat in a corner, dazed at all the finery, perhaps homesick for a world he'd just realized existed. Who knows what was spoken between them that night? But it made the soldier desert his squad and find work in a neighboring town as a farmhand. It made the sheltered girl sneak from the grounds of her estate to meet her new love in the woods. The result of those nights together was my grandmother.

By THE TIME my mother got to this part of the story, we were parked in the driveway. No one made a move to get out of the car, though my gas-conscious father had turned the engine off. As the warmth faded from the car, we huddled more deeply in our coats.

WHEN THE TOWN'S richest daughter became pregnant, the villagers quickly remembered that the American hero was black. He had to flee the countryside, and the girl was sent to a home for unwed mothers. After my grandmother was born, the family used its pull to arrange for their daughter's bastard to be shipped to an orphanage in America. Nana adopted my grandmother and raised her in New Jersey. She received a comfortable, middle-class upbringing, rare in those days for a child of color, not to mention one raised by an unmarried woman. But it wasn't France, it wasn't in a mansion, and it wasn't with the parents who would have looked upon her as their love made visible.

By the time my mother finished talking, we'd almost finished getting ready for bed. My brother and I brushed our teeth slowly, the weight of heritage heavy on our pajama-d shoulders.

But why hadn't the French girl and the soldier just run away to America and gotten married and lived happily ever after? we wanted to know, as we were tucked in.

"Because her parents would never have forgiven her," my mother said. "And family is the most important thing in the world. It's too bad for us, though, isn't it? Imagine how different our lives would be."

When the lights went out, Stewie and I were silent. Clearly, the world didn't work at all. Else we would be living in a castle so huge we wouldn't have to hear our parents fight about money. We would ride ponies to school and have our own rooms. I hated sharing a room with Stewie and pretended he didn't exist when we were in there.

"Guess what?" I whispered across the room. "I was supposed to be a princess. So from now on, you have to call me Princess."

"Oh yeah?" he whispered back. "Then you gotta call me Princess, too."

WHEN THE SKY lightens, I figure it's time to get a move on. "*Levez-vous.*" I poke Luciano. He jumps up with military quickness and begins dismantling the bed. I watch him from the ground, feeling heavy-headed and grouchy.

Footsteps. It's a jogger coming around the bend, dialing a number on his cell phone. Even from this distance, I can see where he's combed over his bald spot.

I unzip my bag. When the jogger nears us and finally looks up, he sees a young woman in an argyle sweater waiting patiently for the vagrant in the wall to accept her donation of bread and cheese, the same provisions Luciano begged for me the night before. The man nods to me as he passes. Luciano is busy folding up the blanket. I don't know if he's seen the jogger. If he has, he doesn't indicate. When he's stowed everything away, he asks me if I want to go to a place that offers free showers. Suddenly, I feel so dirty I have to agree.

Being poor, in my mind, requires a low profile, just like crying in public requires sunglasses. Luciano doesn't seem to think there's anything shameful about our situation. After our showers, as we munch our bread and cheese, he speaks loudly of his plans for the day.

"I know a place for people who have nothing. Sometimes they give you money, a place to stay. We can get ourselves some clean clothes." A fur-clad woman is walking a tiny dog toward us. I turn away from the expression on her face.

"I have clothes," I whisper testily. I want to think, but Luciano won't allow silence. He talks and sings and bangs on the walls, calling out greetings to people, who quicken their pace. He takes my arm and swings me into a building: a lot of dead-eyed people standing around, holding little plastic cups. A bulletin board in the center of the room pleads HELP US TO HELP YOU. No one is reading it.

What is this place?

He shrugs. It's a lot of things, but in the mornings, it gives away free coffee.

I storm out, ignoring the new pain in my foot, struggling to break into a run. He catches up with me easily. Okay, so I don't like coffee. We'll just catch the Métro to this agency and . . .

"With what? Catch the Métro with what money? I'm not hopping the turnstile."

No problem, we'll just ask somebody for money. It won't kill us.

Just then, I realize the night before would've been the perfect opportunity to freeze to death. All I would have had to do was let go of that blanket.

But I didn't. I held on—I don't know for what, but not for this.

"I have an idea," I say brightly. "Why don't you go the agency by yourself, and we'll meet at the Pont des Arts at one? I'm just too scared to go into the Métro without a ticket."

He eyes me, drumming a bass line on his pant legs. "If you aren't there, if you leave me, what will you do? You have no one. You can't speak good French. The police will throw you in jail." He's bopping now, tapping his feet.

"I know. I'll be there. One o'clock. Where else would I go?"

I leave him in front of the Pont Neuf Métro station and cross the street to study the *plan de quartier* so he won't see which direction I go.

The eyes of the woman at the free showers, the way she stared into the mirror while water ran over her toothbrush—that'll never be my life. I can't guarantee much at this point, but I'll make sure of that.

Suddenly I realize I don't want to kill myself. I can't kill myself. Is that the same thing? Right now, wondering that is a luxury I don't have.

After a few minutes, I can concentrate on reading the map. I turn to see where I am in relation to it. Across the street stands Luciano, three steps into the station. He holds his head just above the railing, staring like he knows he's never going to see me again.

GAMES TO PLAY WHEN YOU'RE HOMELESS

OBJECT: Breeze through the three stages of itinerancy while looking cool and collected in a pair of shades!

REQUIREMENTS: pair of shades

HIDE AND WEEP

STAGE 1: DESPAIR

Quickly don your sunglasses whenever you feel tears coming on. You can weep freely behind them, and passersby will be none the wiser. Just be sure not to let mouth or shoulders tremble.

SCORING: If tears fall beneath the frames, you lose!

HIDE AND SLEEP
STAGE 2: EXHAUSTION

You're done crying. Your eyes won't even stay open that long.
Now those sunglasses will really come in handy! (Just make sure
there's sun, or at least daylight.) Be the mysterious person on the Métro,
the sunbather at parks, the cool commuter at bus stops!

SCORING: Be careful not to tumble over in your sleep.
If you wake up on the sidewalk in front of a bench with half the
people on the Champs-Elysées staring down at you, you lose!

HIDE
STAGE 3: THERE'S NO NAME FOR THIS

If you are trudging down the street, past tears, past exhaustion,
and you notice people gaping at you, put the glasses back on.
It means your eyes are not good to see.

INTERVIEW WITH A ROCK STAR

CH. 09

I 've been taking it easy on my left foot since yesterday. Now the right starts to hurt as well, and my heart begins to pound. The nights of wandering have taken their toll. I stop and lean against a wall, trying to work out the cramps, trying to figure out what I'll do if I can't get around anymore. I have always taken to the streets, both for my sanity and to avoid the crowded subways and buses of New York. I've often stood for hours in bookstores or spent a day with wet socks. But there's always been an end to it, a time to rest. Being homeless is one long walk; now it's beginning to feel as if I've come to the end of the road.

Yet, as always, appearance is everything. Just across the bridge from where I stand is Notre Dame. While in better days I eschewed crowds, the more desperate I begin to feel, the more I take comfort in them. My plan is to make my way over to the cathedral's square, slip my hands into the pockets of my jeans, and whistle soundlessly as I pretend to study the mobs of tourists snapping pictures of the church on this brisk October day. Every step I take toward it, however, feels like a car is running over that foot. My upper lip begins to sweat. I think of my bed from last night, in the hole. I've been walking ten minutes and haven't even reached the middle of the bridge yet.

A stout, older couple is coming toward me, walking almost as slowly as I. The man has his arm around the woman's waist, his fingers tracing her hip lightly, up and down. The woman has her head on the man's shoulder, eating one of the long baguette sandwiches that have become the push and pull of my dreams. The sandwich is half-wrapped in paper, but I can see pieces of mayonnaise-slathered tomato, lettuce, slices of seasoned meat. It looks like it'll last forever. First the woman takes a bite; then she holds it up to the man. She seems to know instinctively when he has swallowed the last bit, before offering it to him again. They don't look at anything at all.

They could be anywhere, I think scornfully, turning my back on them. The Seine is as black as the coming night. If God himself were in there, you wouldn't be able to tell.

When I finally make it to a bench, facing the river, I drop into it, lowering myself with my hands. For the first time, it strikes me, the futility of struggling to get from one place to another, when I have nowhere to go. Stillness, however, requires a self-possession I lack these days. If I sit somewhere and do nothing, I'm afraid people will know why. After three days, I've acquired a few poses:

1) Time Out for Nature! This calls for gazing at my surroundings with a peaceful expression.

2) Let's Get Organized! Here, I study my day planner with a pensive expression, occasionally drawing a flower in the blank squares of October.

3) The Reader. During which I take out the same paperback I finished days ago, careful to hold it right side up.

Today I decide to give myself a treat and just look homeless.

Weighing your options takes no time when you have none. I have no money, no working phone card, no numbers on me to call collect if I could figure out how. But I can't do this anymore. Twice this morning, I drifted into oncoming traffic, thinking that since the cars were moving, I could too. The cold is eating me. I can no longer take a step without pain. There will be no surviving this night. True, that was my previous intention, but now I don't want to die. I just want to sleep.

So I'll have to sleep with someone. I'll have to go home with a stranger, and not because he has beautiful eyes or a mouth that sends shivers through me. I just want to be warm and quiet, all alone in a room with no eyes. If I have that for just one night, I know I can figure something out, get myself out of this. It's no big deal, I tell myself. Women have been doing this, as the saying goes, since Eve bit into that apple. My stomach contracts. I think of apples.

"*Il fait froid.*" I open my eyes. A man in a brown trench coat is passing by.

"*Ouais,*" I agree listlessly.

"You are American?" he asks in English. How can they tell? I don't profess to be fluent, but I think I at least have "yeah" down pat. The man has slowed his step only a bit, but when I nod, he stops.

"You are here on holiday? You look like you've been doing a lot of sightseeing."

"I've been walking for days."

"Have you seen the Eiffel Tower?" Even Parisians themselves, he informs me, never tire of their beautiful city. There's so much to see here, so much to do. He takes out a wilted handkerchief and blows his nose, shaking his head back and forth as he does.

"Allow me to guess." He waves the handkerchief at me. "This is your first time out of the country."

"I was in Italy for three months. I worked there."

"Ah, *bella* Italia! And why did you leave?"

"I guess I was just sick of it."

"Surely you've heard what Goethe once said: 'One who is tired of Italy is tired of life.'"

"That wasn't Goethe. That was Samuel Johnson. And he said it about London."

"Oh." The man dabbed at his nose. "What did Goethe say, again?"

"I don't know. Probably lots of things."

He is leaning against the wall, studying me. "I bet all the men loved you there. I bet they were all like, *'Ciao, bella!'* and pinched your bottom. They love the black women over there, as do I."

I look up at him. I've been talking to him because if I'm talking, I'm not thinking. Now I realize he's what I've been thinking of. As if he's read my mind, he gives his nose a quick blow and stands up straight, his eyes never leaving my face. He has a shaved, bald head with three pimples on the left side. His eyes beneath his thick glasses slope toward his nose. He's shaped exactly like a thumb.

"Do you have a cigarette?" I ask. He smiles.

I WAS STILL in grade school the day cigarettes became my portable god. We had parked next to a motorcycle while my dad ran into the supermarket, a place my mother avoided like the plague. The supermarket, with its family-size packs of ground beef, housewives steering shopping carts like tanks, and kids screaming for candy. My mother told him that whenever she was in one, she knew that her life was ruined. So she waited for him in the car. Stewie and I, who had done the aforementioned ruining, waited in the back.

The bike must've been illegally parked; I remember that my father complained as he pulled into his spot. Either way, a cop came along presently, wrote something on a piece of paper, and left it on the motorcycle's windshield. When I asked my mother about it, she told me he'd gotten a ticket.

"A ticket? A ticket to where?" I yelled, craning my neck to see where the cop had gone. "I want a ticket, too!"

My mother turned around to face me. "It's not a good ticket, stupid," she said wearily. "It's a ticket for being an asshole."

My father was getting into the car with a paper sack of groceries. He turned to me as well and quickly corrected, "The owner of that motorcycle's not being polite, kiddo. So the policeman gave him a ticket, and now he has to give the city some of his money, to help him learn better manners."

Just then, a big man with wild hair came sauntering up to the bike. He wore sunglasses, even though it was a cloudy winter afternoon. You could tell just by the way he walked that he hadn't gotten smacked for getting holes in his jeans.

I don't know if the man was aware that a family of four was watching him from their car, but when he saw the ticket, he stopped. He slipped a box of cigarettes from his back pocket. It was a red-and-white box, like the kind that would hold candy. He took out a thick lighter, made a careless gesture with his wrist, produced fire. He lit the cigarette, his eyes on the ticket. A breeze kicked up, and it began to flutter on the windshield in an imperious way. Before getting on his bike and starting the engine, the man removed it. As he started off, his hand came out and the ticket, now crumpled into a ball, flew away. It disappeared somewhere between the grey parking lot and the grey sky.

My parents whirled around quickly, as though one of us had farted. They turned to see me with the window rolled down, head craned out into the frosty winter air, the better to watch the asshole go.

"That man is going to get in big trouble," my mother told me. Her voice sounded stern but nervous, as though she were afraid the biker would hear her and come roaring back.

"Nuh-uh," I scoffed. "Not if they don't catch him."

"Well, let's hope they do, for his sake," my father said primly. "That man wasn't even wearing a helmet."

The roar of the motorcycle's engine faded away. They made me roll the window back up, then turned back to begin the painstaking task of examining the grocery receipt. Had all the coupons been rung up?

Would the two boxes of Hamburger Helper overwhelm the one package of ground chuck? Should potato chips be added?

In the back seat, I was seized with a choking, formless terror. My parents had always told me I could do whatever I wanted once I was a grownup. But they were grownups. If they were happy with their lives, they did a better job of hiding it than they did our Christmas presents. The motorcycle man, however, he was free in a way that my parents weren't, maybe never had been. I wanted to be just like that when I grew up. Except not with the beard.

Senior year in high school was the first time I would smoke a real cigarette. But on that winter afternoon, I made a *v* with my fingers and pretended I had one. When I breathed out, it was so cold, my breath came out like smoke. I felt like I was saving my own life.

THE MAN SAYS he knows a better place to talk. I tell him my feet hurt—all that sightseeing. Not to worry, he assures me as he takes my arm. We'll take it slow. He believes, in fact, in taking many things very slow, very gentle.

Paris is full of this: young black girls holding on to the arms of white-haired white men. Some of the girls I've seen look away quickly if they see someone staring. Some of them return the gaze, flicking their hair or hips saucily. I put on my sunglasses. I'm not one of them—I'm a rock star.

His name is Bertram. He is forty-five, a research librarian. He is single but not lonely, not at all. He has a lot of friends, travels frequently. On Wednesdays, he plays racquetball.

Oh, really, I used to teach tennis in America? Do I know who his favorite player is? Venus Williams. He also enjoys the American music, especially the Clan du Wu-Tang, Snoopy Dogg-Dogg.

As slow as we start walking, my teeth chatter with pain. We have walked up some steps onto a dusty, gravelly walkway. In three days, I've lost so much weight that I have trouble keeping up the jeans that were gelato-snug in Italy. I worry the bottoms are going to drag in the dust and look grey and homeless. Bertram is telling me about Africa. He's never been, but he's heard such wonderful things about it. Shall we sit here?

He's pointing to two of the green metal chairs that line the walkway, directly beneath a giant hunk of statue: muscular legs, penis, a broken wing. On the perimeter of the walkway are busts: brown, black, and cream heads, staring with no eyes. On the opposite side is a massive, headless man, the tiny head of a woman engraved beneath his chest, a leering Medusa at his crotch. In the distance, the Louvre stretches out its wings in an elegant stone embrace. Farther into the park, people stroll along paths that frame a maze of lawn, lush as carpet. There's a fountain where children set little boats to sail with sticks. There are statues of angels wrestling and of armless men staring at the ground. In the center of it all is a giant mask—a man's face, more beautiful than that of any person I've ever seen, and all about us are wildflowers, wildflowers of such color and profusion, all yearning toward the pale, October sun.

This place, I wonder. *How could this place and my life be in the same world?*

"The Jardin des Tuilleries," Bertram whispers moistly into my ear. "Do you like it?" When I nod, he smiles and turns my chair in the dust to face him. "You're very young, aren't you? How old—twenty-two, twenty-three?"

"Um … okay."

Do I have a boyfriend in America? I haven't had many boyfriends, have I? He can always tell. It's such a shame about young girls like me. He sits back in his chair and sighs, then gasps and begins coughing violently. The white handkerchief flutters out of his pocket.

"What's a shame?"

"That young girls like you, in the full bloom of youth"—he gestures to the flowers—"are wasted on boys who don't know how to treat them, to show them what the world offers." He reaches over and picks up one of my hands. "My dear, you are so cold!" His fingers are short and fat, like those little sausages that come in the cans. Vienna sausages. My mouth begins to water.

"I never thought of it like that."

"Of course you haven't, my dear. Because romance—a good dinner, a fine wine, even the act of love itself—it's an art that can only be acquired with time, no?" I nod solemnly. Maybe he has some food in his pocket.

The school kids, the handsome older couples, the tourists filming the flowers—I feel like everyone is looking at us. He has both my hands between his now. I can't take them away. It's the warmest they've been in days.

"What is strange for me," he is saying, "is that right now, I am without a woman. I have no one in my life. It doesn't happen often, my dear, let me assure you." He frees my hands so he can attend to his nose. That handkerchief has had it. "But one must wait, of course, for the right woman to come along. And when she does, she may not feel *you* are the right one, may not like your face, your physique." He points to the statue of the muscular, headless angel. "That's what I look like under my coat," he quips.

"But if the woman really is the right one," I say, "she'll look past all that and judge you on who you are, not what you look like."

Bertram becomes still as he looks at me. "You are very wise."

I turn away. A young couple, matching leather jackets and tousled curls, are strolling hand in hand among the flowers. The boy steps in front of the girl, tilts her chin with one finger, kisses her softly on the mouth. You get the feeling he doesn't do things like that often. At first, the girl's hands are arcs of surprise, frozen by her waist. Then they go up, past his face, seeking the shelter of his hair.

"My dear, is something wrong?"

"Oh, no! My eyes always get teary when it's cold." It's windy, too. A breeze picks up suddenly, blowing his hand onto my knee.

"I would like to see you again. Can I call you?"

"Well, I'd love to. See you, I mean. But I don't know where I'll be or how you could call."

"Well, where are you staying?"

"I'm not staying anywhere. It's funny, really"—I give a plucky laugh—"but I'm a little short on cash at the moment."

"What do you mean?"

"It was one of those crazy things that happen when you travel. My money got stolen in Termini Station in Rome. I haven't had any place to stay since I got here."

"But can't you call someone?"

"I don't know anyone here, and ... well, it's funny that you should mention Africa before, because that's where my parents are ... on a safari." (I have to bite my lip at the thought of my mother in the African bush.) "They'll be home in a few days; in the meantime"—I smile bravely—"I sure am getting to see a lot of Paris!"

"But my darling, where do you sleep?"

"I don't."

"How do you eat?"

"Oh, that." I wave my hand. "After the first twenty-four hours, you stop feeling hungry. These statues remind me of Rome.... "

"Wait, just a second, *cherie*. Let me think," he says to my breasts. Then, lightbulb: "I know! You can stay with me."

"But . . . but we hardly know each other." This elicits a hearty chuckle and a knee squeeze.

"I think we are very fortunate to have *found* each other." Suddenly, he frowns. "But my dear, you have no money? How does one have no money?" The hand slips from my knee as though my circumstances were contagious.

"It's my fault, actually." I shake my head. "I was just about to board the train in Rome, when I saw the cutest little girl wandering through the crowd. She was all alone, crying. I bent down to ask her where her mother was. All of the sudden, she stopped crying and ran away. When I turned around, the front part of my backpack was open. She was part of a group of gypsies. They got everything, all my money. All I had left was a ticket to Paris. Not too smart for a girl from New York."

Bertram leans over and touches my face. With the handkerchief hand. "You are very sweet," he whispers, looking contrite for having doubted me. "Listen, my love, I have to go back to work now. But let's meet tonight, shall we? Around eight?" He stands up, but my feet cramp at the thought.

"I'll wait for you here."

"For three hours? *Mais non!* You are already freezing. Have you ever heard of Pompidou?" I haven't. "Georges Pompidou—it's a very big library. They have quite the English-language section there. We can meet at the front entrance. And here." He is pressing something against my palm. "Get yourself something to eat. But not too much, I want you hungry when you see me." He slides his hands down to my hips as I stare at the fiver he has given me. It's money. I'm holding it. I'm holding it with both hands. How strange, to love something so much that you know you'll give away. I can feel him watching me. *Say something.*

"Four hours, huh? That's a lot of reading."

"Well, you know, they also have free Internet."

I almost drop the money.

I try to keep my mind on my mission as I race to the library. All the people I'll email, what I'll tell them about my situation. What I'll do once I get my hands on some real dough. I have to make some plans beyond sleep, a shower, and a twenty-piece box of Chicken McNuggets.

But all I can think is, *I don't have to do this. I don't have to do this.* I think of Bertram's hands on my hips, his kiss goodbye still glistening on my cheek. I begin to shiver all over again, as though I've been rescued from some horrible, runny-nosed beast. I can feel every cobblestone beneath my feet as I walk, but the pain is a benediction.

At the supermarket, I buy a box of Pim's cookies. Jam and chocolate and cake vibrate in different frequencies of sweetness throughout my body. I finish half the box in the checkout line.

At Pompidou, the librarian hands me my computer station number on a slip of paper. I have thirty minutes; no liquids, and there is, of course, no email access.

"*Répétez, s'il vous plaît.* That last part?" The Internet is for research purposes only, she tells me. It's impossible to access one's email from here.

Of course. It wasn't meant to be. It's not like I can ask my friends for plane fare back home, or even that I have any place to go back home to.

And if she's so broke, I can just picture people thinking, *what in the world is she doing in Paris, of all places?* What could I have written? "Please send me a little money so I can eat a few meals, sleep a few nights indoors, steel myself for an existence I'm beginning to realize I have no way out of"?

Do I still want to use the computer? the librarian asks me. I shake my head. Ask where the bathroom is. Take the elevator to the second floor. Go into the first stall. Throw up.

THE LIARS' CLUB

CH. 10

Châtelet, where Pompidou is located, abounds with cheap Internet cafés. On my way over, I pass several. With the €4 from Bertram that I still have, I could write everyone I know about my situation and still have money to check my email for the next two days. But that's not one of the choices given to me, and it seems like I can't come up with any of my own. For the last few months, along with the crying spells and the insomnia, there has existed a black cloud of confusion that lies heavily upon my brain. Before any completed, complex thought towers a wall against which my mind slumps in despair. All I know is that in two and a half hours, I'm going to have to sleep with a fat man. A fat man with a cold. I feel weak. I feel sick. I need a cigarette.

The hangout at Georges Pompidou is the second-floor terrace. Kids gather there in groups, eating snacks from the kiosk, chatting on cell phones. Everyone there is a student, or as poor as one, so a feeling of scruffy unity hangs in the hash-scented air. It's a good place to bum a smoke.

Still, one has to exercise caution. I'm always careful not to look as if I've come out here for the express purpose of getting a free ciga-rette. I stride purposefully to the terrace, stopping in the center, look-ing left to right. After that, I glance at my watch. Now everyone thinks I'm waiting for someone. I move to a vantage point close to the door, as though this person is coming any minute. Occasionally, I check my watch with a pressed-lipped sigh of impatience. Don't people have any respect for time?

Meanwhile, I'm scoping out a potential donor. I can't approach any large group of smokers—I'd have to suffer the scornful looks of the people whose friend I cornered. Nor the old men who skulk in the shadows, eyeing the lithe young girls. No girls, period. I try to zero in on a studious-looking guy, one who seems slightly uneasy in this boisterous setting. And I always offer 50¢. They never take it, but it works like a charm.

It's strange, I think, as I scan the terrace, that gypsies popped into my mind as I explained my predicament to Bertram. After the night my mother told Stewie and me the truth about our grandmother, we never forgot for a second that we were descended from royalty. The secrecy we'd vowed to uphold, however, made us as clannish as a pack of thieves: distrustful of a world that had kept us from our rightful place in life, dis-dainful of its rules, and, especially as the years went by, so restless within the chokehold of lower-middle-class-ness that we'd rather go anywhere, be anywhere, so long as it wasn't home.

Even before Stewie and I were told the truth, however, what children were treated more like royalty than we? In the mornings after we'd gotten dressed, we'd drift into the living room, where my mother would have made up the couches with sheets, blankets, and pillows. We'd go to our respective couch-beds and slip under the covers to await breakfast, which was always served to us on TV trays. Propped up on pillows, we breakfasted on Lipton tea and ramen noodles, singing along sleepily to *Josie and the Pussycats.*

"Poor babies, they shouldn't have to get up this early every fucking morning," my mother would say, patting our groggy heads. Quite often, over my father's protests, we didn't. If it was too rainy or too snowy or too Monday, we were permitted to stay home, provided we entertain ourselves in our room until early afternoon, when my mother officially rose for the day. We had delicate palates and were never bothered with pesky things like vegetables. My mother had her own set of nutritional guidelines, which dictated that in the house would always be snacks from three different food groups: chips, ice cream, and Hostess.

We never had any household chores. When my mother or father vacuumed, they'd apologize for the noise. We'd still roll our eyes, one of us getting off the couch to turn up the volume on the TV. We were never allowed to go outside to play with the neighborhood kids as they tore around on their bikes or jumped rope. Stewie and I would watch them from the window of our third-floor apartment, as though from a turret on a castle so high, it touched the clouds.

We were always together, in our own little kingdom where my mother reigned supreme and Stewie and I were treasured heirs. My father was the faithful servant, allowed to sit at the table with us as long as he served first and cleaned up afterward.

Books, more than anything, provided a constant escape. During the winters, a news alert would often warn about an approaching snowstorm. When this happened, everyone in New Jersey would rush out of the house to stock up on salt and shovels at the hardware store and snatch every edible item off supermarket shelves. This worked out perfectly for my family, since the first place my parents, Stewie, and I would go was the library, and we'd have it all to ourselves.

"Get no more than two," my mother would whisper after us as we slipped off like fugitives toward the shelves. "We'll meet at the checkout in about five minutes." Half an hour later, all four of us would come staggering back to the rendezvous point, books piled high to our chins. My brother favored Choose Your Own Adventure books and thick trilogies that featured dragons who spoke and warriors who didn't have to. My dad liked the Civil War, as most dads seem to, and horror stories that kept him up half the night. My mother went for romances, or any novel that featured a young woman with no husband and no kids. I liked everything: Judy Blume, biographies of unstable artists, stories about families with lots of children, adopted or otherwise. It was fascinating to read about adults who actually liked having children.

We spent hours in the bookstore of every mall we went to, and this was before they had cafés. The conversation at dinner was often about books, and a recounting of Harriet the Spy was listened to as attentively as one of a bio about Mata Hari. We talked about characters as though they were our friends, quoted beautiful lines with as much pride as if we had written them ourselves. After dinner, we'd gather in the living room to watch prime-time TV, but we'd each have a book to get us through the commercials.

During the closing credits we'd often look up and laugh, realizing a program had gone off without our realizing. When only one of us noticed, that person would get up, walk quietly past the bent heads of the rest of the family, shut off the TV, and go back to his or her book.

As she grew fatter, my mother withdrew from the few girlfriends she had. Having gotten pregnant with me shortly after she graduated high school, she'd only ever worked at a few entry-level jobs. Though she'd vowed to get a job after Stewie started school, her burgeoning weight became a shield against the threat of ever going to work again. My dad wasn't allowed to have friends until he started making more money. Certainly, Stewie and I couldn't let our friends from private or parochial school see where we lived. So it was always just us. Seated around the dining room table, we played Scrabble and Uno and Trouble and Hungry Hungry Hippos. The last was a game where you pushed a lever at the back of your hippo to make its mouth open and swallow as many marbles off the board as possible. (We tried not to laugh when Stewie scooped up marbles by hand and shoved them into his hippo's mouth so he would win.) We also played chess and checkers and a game with no name that consisted of taking a larger word, like "transportation" or "notebook" or "zebra," and making as many smaller ones as you could from it. On weekends, when most people visit family or friends, the four of us got in the car and drove down the highway until we came to a town with an interesting name. That's how we discovered Succasunna, whose quiet and uncrowded multiplex became our official movie theater.

Only assholes, my mother told us, paid all that money in movie theaters for overpriced popcorn and sodas. Since we were definitely smarter than assholes, we would get our candy and chips at a nearby five-and-dime and sneak them in. This worked perfectly until midway through the movie, when we'd all find ourselves thirsty. No problem— only an asshole wouldn't have thought to sneak in four cans of soda as well. In our rush to reach the theater on time, however, we'd skip lunch, never knowing if traffic would make the trip one hour or two. What kind of parents would stuff their kids full of Junior Mints and Cheetos before feeding them a balanced meal? We began to stop at McDonald's or White Castle first. In the summer, my mother's purse held most of our booty. In the winter, we'd squirrel everything under our coats and waddle in, lumpy as snowmen.

As soon as we got into our seats, we'd look around at all the suckers with their giant, watered-down sodas and boxes of stale candy. As soon as the lights dimmed, however, it was our turn to be stared at. We tried to be as quiet as possible, but pretty soon the theater would be filled with the smell of oil and vinegar from our Blimpie subs or french fries from Burger King. There'd be a hushed whisper of "Ma, could you pass me my dippin' sauce?"

We tried to fit in the majority of our meal prep during the previews. These seemed to get longer as I grew older, from one or two to so many that the four of us could eat the entire pepperoni pizza we'd snuck in inside an empty Toys"R"Us bag. Our parents had warned us that if we were caught, we'd get kicked out of the theater; this made walking through the lobby almost as exciting as the movie itself. Surely the concession workers could tell that the roses in my cheeks were from the boxes of six-piece Chicken McNuggets I held under my sweater.

As the youngest, Stewie was usually in charge of small stuff, like condiments and paper utensils. One day, after he pleaded for a promotion, my parents put him in charge of our four cans of root beer.

From the moment we walked into the theater, though, the kid was all wrong. Instead of striding in coolly, he hunched over like Quasimodo. He lurched past the other moviegoers, a wide and terrified look in his eyes each time he lost sight of us. When he finally stood straight up to hand the usher his ticket, the four cans of soda fell out of his coat and rolled down the lobby toward the theater.

"Those aren't mine!" my brother yelled. The rest of the Royal Family, leaking McDonald's fries and ketchup packets, scurried after them.

"CAN I GIVE you fifty cents for a cigarette?" I can say it in four languages, shoulders slightly raised, two front teeth toying with my bottom lip.

The guy I've chosen jumps back, as though I've poked him with a cattle prod. He has an unlit cigarette dangling from his lips. Very pink lips, I notice.

"You are American?" *Merde.* "You don't have to pay," he says with a little smile. He hands me the cigarette from his mouth. "I actually asked for this one."

"Oh! Then take it back. I'm sorry." I hold it out to him, my fingers closed around it in a death grip.

"No, no. One moment." He disappears into the crowd, walking stiffly. His shoulders are very broad.

He returns, couldn't find another. I offer to share mine. "Really?" he smiles. He has a way of licking his *l*'s. He's something else—not French. I ask him.

"Guess," he says, standing up straight. He runs a hand through his black hair. I could just eat him. Actually, with the way things have been, I could eat anyone on the terrace.

"Spanish? Greek?"

He's grinning. "I'm from Tunisia." He's a math tutor, a third-year engineering student. He's the only one on the terrace in a three-piece suit.

What am I doing here? Oh, loving Paris, exploring my options, sleeping under a bridge.

His name is Asad. He tells me he knows a lot of students who would pay good money for English lessons. We exchange contact information before parting. Of course, this is so he can ask me out. I won't even be able to check my email to see when he does. It doesn't matter; people who go on dates live in another world, a world where you shower every day, eat regular meals, don't fall asleep while walking. But I'll keep his number, take it out every once in a while. It'll give me something to think about, imagining what might have been.

I DIDN'T REALLY grow up in Newark; I grew up in the car. Once we'd left the apartment, we spent all of ten minutes in the ghetto. Five minutes when we walked to the car, five minutes walking back. (Sometimes even quicker if it was after dark.) We shopped for groceries, went to the mall, even did our laundry, in nicer towns. On Sundays, we took rides through the country, past farms, through tiny burgs that still had white clapboard churches and general stores. If we passed cows grazing by the side of the road, I'd watch their expressions of bemusement as my dad stopped the car, stuck his head out the window, and went, "Moo! Moo! Moo?" Not another car around for miles, but I'd still slump down in my seat, embarrassed.

"Oh God," my mother would groan as we piled into the car after a day of errands. "I can't go back to the ass crack of New Jersey. Let's go somewhere else first, so I can forget that we have to go home."

So my dad would take us just a few exits down the highway and we'd enter another world. We'd drive slowly through the leafy, wealthy neighborhoods of Essex County. We would take in the grand homes nestled on lush lawns. Even the swing sets were more impressive: tall, wooden structures with tree houses and wavy slides. Tire swings hung from the branches of towering oaks that looked as though they could swing you up to the sky. At night, if we drove slowly enough, we could see inside other people's houses.

"Why don't they pull their curtains shut?" I'd ask.

"The same reason they don't have fences around their yards: because when you have enough money, you can afford to live by nice people who won't peek into your house to see what they can steal." My mother sighed. "You don't have to be afraid.

"Notice the bookcases. Do you guys see that sometimes they have entire walls full of nothing but books?" She would turn around to the back seat to make sure we were paying attention. "And look at the furniture. Almost none of these homes has very much of it. They have a few nice pieces and a lot of empty space. Not cluttered with crap and knickknacks all over the place."

"Like our house," Stewie quipped.

We would whisper on these rides, as though our car were creeping through a museum rather than along hushed, residential streets. Sometimes we'd catch a glimpse of a family sitting down to eat in a plum-colored dining room, a child frolicking with a dog on a vast front lawn. The air smelled different here: crisp in the winter, sweet and heavy on warm summer nights.

"Kids, imagine what our lives would be like if we lived here," my mother said on one of these drives. Her voice was soft and once-upon-a-time.

"We would run outside after breakfast and play in our tree house."

"We would have an upstairs and a downstairs."

"We could walk to school."

"And have friends over to play."

"We could have Twinkies whenever we wanted to."

My mother snapped out of her reverie. "What the hell does that have to do with it?"

I shrugged. "I'm hungry."

"We've been driving around for an hour," my dad said, eyeing the gas tank.

"Fine, take us home so you can make us dinner, you pussy! That's all you're good for. You can't even give my kids the fucking life they deserve."

"Can I have a Twinkie?"

"Shut up, you little pig!" Then back to my dad. "Don't my kids deserve better than the life you've given them? Don't they?"

"Yes," my father answered. It sounded like a sigh. We would all sigh as the car descended from those tree-lined streets back to the litter-laden sidewalks of our neighborhood. Boom boxes blaring, women in rollers spilled over open windows as they looked down at gangs of men swilling beer on the corner and unsupervised children darting out into the middle of the street. In Newark, it always smelled the same. None of it seemed quite real, and when we finally got out, I tried to forget I'd ever lived there at all.

Harder to forget was my first concept of home: a place you circle slowly, peering in, studying every detail, dreaming of the day when you can leave where you are and your real life will begin.

STUDENTS OFTEN FALL asleep at the long tables in Pompidou, heads dropped over textbooks and Penguin Classics. I know that if I allow myself to doze off, I'll sleep so long it'll be more of a folk tale than a nap. I struggle to read as my eyes flutter and shut, heavy as wet towels.

I check my watch. In thirty minutes, I'm going to go home with a man who has little sausage fingers. I think I've caught his cold; my throat hurts and I feel chilled inside. My head begins to pound with such an ache, it seems as though the entire library is throbbing. I look around, half expecting to see the books go limp and slide off the shelves, for librarians to topple off their prim little chairs, screaming in pain.

At ten to eight, I rise to go. My feet hurt even more after I've been off them for a while. I notice people watching me as I make my way to the escalator, can almost hear them wondering, *Who limps with both feet?*

I bum a cigarette by the exit. It tastes horrible. Since I'm getting sick, it'll do me good to spend a few nights indoors, have some decent meals. I'm doing the right thing—that's why I feel so bad. Doing the right thing is always hard, always makes you throw up.

At five minutes to eight, he comes out of the exit—Asad, the cute guy who gave me a cigarette. When he sees me, he brightens like a little boy and walks quickly toward me. He's like someone who's never been hurt. I want to touch him.

"Hey! What are you doing out here?"

I give my first honest answer since I came to Paris: "I don't know." The wind picks up and I shiver, forgetting not to fight it.

THE WAY
THEY WALK
IN TUNISIA

CH. 11

T
he first night I spend with Asad, I have a dream. I'm lying on my
stomach on a petal-strewn cliff. The flowers all about me are a soft
pink. Up above, the night sky is doing some wondrous twinkling
thing. Instead of stars, fat raindrops hang suspended in the sky. Nestled in
the valley below is a cluster of sleepy little cottages. I long to hold a bit of
this place in my hand, though I know I mustn't. I shouldn't even be here.
All this beauty. I scoop up a rose petal. Fake.

Afterward, I let myself remember only the way the dream looked
and made me feel. Make myself forget that to reach the top of the cliff, I
had to crawl on my belly.

ASAD LIVES ON the commuter line, in a small town called Châtenay-
Malabry. The window boxes on the stone houses still flower. He lives in

a single room in student housing, isn't really allowed to have anybody overnight, but . . . when he shrugs, pushing his palms up to the sky, he reminds me of warm nights in Rome. The last two blocks, when my feet really start to hurt, he takes my arm. I haven't slowed or shown any pain; he just knows.

While I shower, he cooks for us: spaghetti and scrambled eggs. Ravenous at first, I'm surprised by how little I can eat.

"Do you like it? Is it okay?" he keeps asking. With his glasses he is handsome; when he takes them off, he looks like that giant, beautiful mask at the Tuilleries.

"I could sleep on the floor," I offer. It's worth a try. This is over the strong, Arabic tea he's brewed.

"I'm not going to eat you," he says. We blush into our teacups.

His room is small and toasty. He gives me a T-shirt, wonders at my keeping my socks on. He covers us with two fuzzy blue blankets. We kiss a little; he fondles my breasts through the shirt. Then we fall asleep.

In the morning, he tells me I can wash my clothes in the sink, and gives me a little blue tub in which to soak my feet.

"Do you want me to go?"

He turns from the computer, smiling. "Not yet."

Late afternoon, from the depths of a dreamless nap, I'm aware of him tiptoeing to the bed. He covers me with the blankets and stands over me for a moment before he goes back to his desk.

It's those first twenty-four hours. God can be so easily confused with His gifts. Even after everything that is to happen later, I can never think of that boy with any bitterness at all.

THAT EVENING, WE have sex for the first time. It's a disaster. He lies on top of me, burying his face in my neck, hardly moving at all. After a few minutes, he pulls me on top, but at that point I've gone dry with disappointment. Afterward, we get dressed and escape his stifling room. We sit across from each other in the empty dining area, an overflowing ashtray between us. Silence and smoke.

"Listen, don't sweat it. The first time usually sucks."

"What?" he snaps. "It didn't suck."

"Okaaay."

"I don't want a girlfriend, you know."

"Who said I was your girlfriend?"

"College is my girlfriend."

He's looking for an internship. On our first morning together, he followed a routine he will continue over the eight days we spend together: He got up promptly at nine and did a Google search, typing very hard on the keyboard. Then he made some phone calls. It was hard to understand what he was saying in his rapid, flawless French, but the calls seemed to end the moment he told the recipient his Arabic name. After a few hours of this, he opened the window in front of his desk, smoking, staring at the leaves.

"You're not even in classes this term. Some love affair." At my words, he flinches, then glares. It's the first time I see it. Not in his eyes, but in the looseness of his mouth—a latent cruelty. Power. He's capable of anything.

The "dining area" is a room adjoining the kitchen and consists of two mismatched picnic tables shoved against each other. Asad swings his long legs over the bench and stalks to a shelf laden with half-opened boxes of pasta and cookies. He returns with a bottle of whiskey and two glasses.

"Is that even your—?" He silences me with a sharp motion. We sit sipping, shuddering from the drink.

"You're ruining the world, you know that? Americans. You're destroying my people."

"What? What the hell are you talking about? What does that have to do with—?"

"Look at Iraq. You've ruined that country. No one works there. The people are starving. Look at Palestine—"

"Listen, I don't see—"

"You wonder why that day in September happened? Your government left them no choice. For years you've given weapons to our oppressors, our enemies. Taught them to fight and left them with nothing to live for—"

"It was the eleventh, asshole!" I jab my finger in his face. "I was there. You don't know. There were pieces of the sky on the ground; men were crying in the streets. That wasn't fighting a government or some holy war. That was people going to work. That was 9/11, and if you don't even know the date, don't fucking mention it."

I pour myself another whiskey. He pours himself one as well. We down them quickly, eyes upon each other. He shudders again, but I don't.

Suddenly, he pushes me along the picnic table bench until I am against the wall. He turns his back on me and lays his head on my lap. My fingers go to his hair. His eyes are pink.

"The only reason you're here is because you have no other place to go. If you had an apartment, you wouldn't be with me."

"That's not true! I don't sleep with guys I don't like. I never have, not once in my life. Do you know how many guys have tried to pick me up since I got here? I stayed in the cold, I stayed hungry, rather than go with them. But you—I liked you the minute I saw you. But if you don't believe me, just tell me to go. I don't want to be here if you think I'm like that."

I hear the wind after I say that, feel the cold blanket of the night. Asad sits up, then reaches behind me to snap off the light. In the darkness, there's nothing but the click of his belt buckle, his hands hiking up my skirt. This time, I'm ready.

The next day, I ask Asad if I can get my luggage. I tell him it's in the youth hostel storage room; I don't tell him the two pieces weigh 120 pounds combined. When we meet afterward at the train station, he blinks several times when he sees it. He carries the biggest bag, my ninety-pound suitcase (I'd packed for a slightly more stable life) over his head, up three flights of stairs.

"You look happy," he says, after I've washed my hair and changed out of the same clothes I've worn for a week.

"You can't be happy when you have nothing. You don't feel like a real person. Know what I mean?"

He thinks for a moment. "No, I don't."

IF I COULD teach English in Rome, I can teach in Paris. He'll help me. He calls some of his students. I work on flyers. We talk about places I could hang them up, pass them out.

When he goes out a few hours each day to tutor, I gather all my own work around: the elementary-French books he's borrowed for me, and my notebook—tiny squares to write in, instead of lines. Socialists. I get one or both of my books on how to teach English. When he comes home, he sees me huddled on the bed, hard at work. But when I'm alone, I push everything onto the floor and lie down. All I want is to rest, to look about me and see walls and ceiling, rather than endless sky.

ON MY THIRD night with Asad, after we make love, he slides between my legs and spreads them wide. He is on his belly. When he blinks, his black lashes sweep his cheeks.

He holds the lips of my vagina open, pokes my clitoris, slides his finger slowly inside me.

I flinch at first, then force myself to relax. I put my hands beneath my head. This seems presumptuous. I let my arms go limp at my sides, feeling myself grow wet all over again at my helplessness.

He looks up. "You are proud of this?"

I shrug. "Yeah."

"You don't have to worry that you don't have work. You have this."

IT'S HARD TO describe him. Sometimes he isn't good looking at all. His nose seems too big, his eyes behind his glasses small and piggy, his upper lip belligerent. Other times he is so wondrous I can't even look at him, only at the pictures my mind has taken. His eyes are black. Women would eat their young to get his lashes. I could write a whole book about his mouth. Most of his countrymen seem to have coarse, straight hair, but his is like black feathers, curling a bit at the ends. He smells better than anyone has a right to, the musk of his aftershave mixed with the sweetness of the boy he still is. When he goes out, I pick up his undershirt hanging on the towel rack. I hold it to my face until I can't breathe.

"This is the way they walk in Tunisia." He drags his feet, the heels of his sandals clomping along the ground. "It's because they're not worried about time." He has two clocks—one big, one bite-size—on the table by his bed. He checks his phone, my watch. He walks very fast, even in the tiny room. When he cleans it, he attacks the books and clothes as though they are his enemies. He studies English for hours, asking me the definitions of words, making me pronounce them over and over again. Whenever I try to speak French, he stops me by the third word, correcting everything I say. Soon, I practice only when I'm in the room alone. "Americans are lazy," he scoffs. He brushes his teeth for longer than anyone I've known, pacing up and down the room, returning to frown into the mirror. I never once hear him spit.

Sometimes I reach out and cuff him. He watches me, his mouth curving up at the ends, waiting for me to do it again. When I do, he grabs for me. He's lean but muscular. I go for his belly, his chin, try to flick him in the ear. We fall to the bed and he presses my arms into the mattress, my legs clenched between his thighs. We are panting, his eyes on my breasts as I try to buck him off.

"All right, I give up."

"I don't believe you."

"I'll be good, I promise." His hands are like iron on my wrists. I can feel his erection lancing my belly.

"You're a little wild, you know that?" he says sternly. I rub myself against him and he smiles.

WHEN I WAS twelve, we moved to Florida for six months—my parents, Stewie, and I, plus all our belongings, weighing down our second-hand Chevrolet. It was the first time I'd ever seen palm trees. I finally got to try everything on the menu at McDonald's. It was hot in the car, and one morning, after we'd spent the night in it, my usually fastidious mother stank. "You stink!" I told my father, and would not let him hug me.

A relative wired us money. We moved out of the car and into a Motel 6. The sixty-watt lightbulbs made us gag, but we were jubilant in the supermarket, buying fruit and deli. I saw a maple Bundt cake, dark and dangerously moist, for $7. I didn't dare ask, but my mother saw me staring and swept it into the cart. We'd all had showers beforehand, and when I hugged her, she smelled wonderful.

Back in our room, I looked up from a book to see my brother holding Fluffy. Fluffy, who'd been my dog since I was nine months old. He no longer lived up to his name, but he was still my prized possession, one of the few toys I'd been allowed to take with us. I was across the orange carpet in two strides, snatching him away in a blur. I think I turned to my mother after that to exchange a look, something like *Will you get a load of this nut?* Something loud happened, and then she was leaning over me, choking me on one of the beds with orange comforters, upon which, my parents had told us, under no circumstances were we ever to put our faces.

Her eyes were big, like a cartoon character's. I could feel her nails digging into my neck as she squeezed tighter, then tighter still. I held on to her arms, terrified of what would happen if I let go.

"You bitch! You whore! You've been nothing but trouble since . . . " Her words were drowned out by a sound like the ocean. Something was wrong. Of course, I'd seen people being choked on TV before, by bad guys in black leather jackets. Scary music would play in the background, and if you were eating potato chips, the pieces you'd been chewing would turn to mush on the roof of your mouth.

But mothers didn't choke. Mothers said things like, "Finish your orange juice. The vitamins are on the bottom." They put fresh clothes in the dryer when you came in from the rain so you'd be toasty and warm right away.

My head bounced like a Ping-Pong ball on the bed as my mother yelled, "Can't he have anything he wants? Can't he have anything he wants?" My father and brother were trees, planted behind her. Then the bigger tree pulled my mother away.

She shrugged out of my father's grasp, smoothing her hair. There was something they'd forgotten at the supermarket, she mused in her telephone voice. I gagged and retched on the bed, curved into a shaking comma. Milk—that was it. When was the last time the kids had had milk?

The three of them left. Such a waste. I was all alone—I could've cried as much as I wanted to, no time limit. Instead, I just lay there, my hands around my throat. From the top of the closet wafted the smell of the maple cake. It was to be, when we all enjoyed it the next day, one of the few baked items that tasted as good as it looked, well worth what it cost.

HE KEEPS STICKING his finger up my ass; it's a problem. When he does it too hard, I yell, "Ow!" and he hisses, "Shh!" and we both sit up, red faced and glaring.

One day when we're nuzzling on the bed, I slide my hand down the back of Asad's pants. I've cut my nails for just this moment.

"*Putain!* What the hell was that?"

"You don't like it?"

"That's my ass, you know." He hikes his pants up, pouting. "I'm not gay."

"You don't have to be gay to like it. The anus is a sensitive area, especially for men." He picks up his smaller clock, a little white square that fits into the palm of his hand.

"Really?" he says to the clock.

"Look at it this way: God gave most animals the desire to mate for only a short time every year. They do it strictly for reproduction. But human beings can do it all the time, and we have all these erogenous zones," he scratches his head, "pleasure spots on our bodies, created for no other reason than to make us feel good. Society has turned sex into a bad thing, because it's dangerous, you know, to have people walking around feeling too good. Happy people are impossible to control. But fuck . . . I mean, forget that." (He's been telling me I curse too much.) "When it comes to sex, you have to do what feels right."

He pulls me back over to him. "You are like . . . how do you say? A psychiatrist. Is that because you're crazy?" From that point on, he lets me put my fingers wherever I want.

Twenty-three-year-olds, they're a different species. Asad can look sleepy, but he's never tired. He drinks shocking quantities of milk. He's ticklish everywhere, even places he didn't know about. He's only two years older than I was when I lost my virginity. I've had a therapist who liked me to talk about my feelings on his lap, a married man who liked to "kidnap" me by tugging me by my ponytail up Park Avenue, and a Greek gangster who made me suck his thumb the whole time we watched *The Godfather: Part II,* but I've never had a boyfriend who was a boy. Sometimes he calls me over to his desk and sticks his head up my shirt. When I peer down at him, his face is like Christmas morning.

His mother has sent him a small cobalt blue teapot in which to brew the strong black tea that reminds me of the Seine at night. One morning, he fills it with water and tea leaves, sets it on the hot plate, then forgets about it until evening. He spends the next day scraping, washing, boiling with vinegar the ruined pot. When he throws it out, I tease him about his intellect. Just a joke, for we both agree on his brilliance.

He turns on me. "It's your fault! I can't think or study or look for a job. There's nothing in my mind but you." Then he laughs at his passion, shaking his head. I try to meet his eyes from my space in the corner of his narrow bed, but he turns away.

Asad's not the only one who can't think. My own mind is a forest these days. I can break down the manys of my situation into only two words: Good. Bad.

It's bad that I don't have a dollar to my name. The day before, I asked to borrow €5 to go to Paris and look for a job. Along with the money, he gave me a look I decided never to relive. Not that I can blame him. Isn't he doing enough—buying all the groceries (more eggs and pasta than I've eaten in all my life), risking eviction by hiding me in his room?

It's bad that I can never go out alone, for the front entrance to the student dorms requires a keycard, which I don't have. Of course, I could always go out and then have Asad call me when he gets back home, but that would require a cell phone, which I also don't have.

It's bad that I have to wait until I'm full to bursting before I dare venture down the hall to the communal bathroom, bad that I can't go into the kitchen at all unless he's there. From breakfast till dinner, I have to content myself with snatches of things he keeps in his linen closet: cookies, the tiny olives from his family's farm in Tunisia that he keeps in a water bottle. I'm always hungry. Once, while doing my French exercises, I tear off a piece of the notebook and chew it. I run to the mirror to show myself how ridiculous I'm being, ridiculous because I'm forgetting the good.

The good is that I have found him, this luminous young animal with his entire future locked away inside him. I start to plan that future in my notebook when I should be conjugating irregular verbs. He'll find an engineering job and start making enough money to move us into a real apartment, where I can cook for him and pee whenever I want. He will, of course, be dependent upon me to advise him. Hasn't he already become incapable of matching his shirt with his pants every morning, to tell if his jokes are funny, to discern whether the "*Ça va?*" of another student we meet in the kitchen is sincere? He needs me far more than I need him.

That night, as I trace the one eyebrow that bridges his forehead (delicate, perfectly arched, but nonetheless one), he tells me how he had no hair at all when he was born, no eyebrows either. "What have you done?" his father yelled at his mother in the hospital. She responded by stealing a black marker from the nurses' station and drawing eyebrows and a few strands of hair on her newborn.

"They shouldn't have acted like that," I whisper. "I bet you looked like an angel." He pulls me close, staring up at the glow-in-the-dark stars on his ceiling. The first night we spent together, I gasped when I saw the stars, just like the ones in my apartment back home, and he laughed and said, "Surprise!"

THE COMMUNAL KITCHEN is shared by the floor's twenty-four inhabitants. The floor is always sticky. At any given time, half the dishes teeter in the sink, and the other half should. The dining area, with the picnic tables, is where Asad likes to fuck. After breakfast, we linger amid the empty yogurt cartons and mugs with tea stains mustaching the rims. "Turn off the light," he tells me, before he's even ashed out his cigarette.

"I heard footsteps. . . . Anyone could come in. . . . Was that a door opening?" I turn off the light. I've learned to wear a skirt to breakfast, to leave my panties behind. As I lower myself onto him, he takes my hands, covers his face with them. I never liked it this way before, two people charging at each other in some moist, wordless battle. Now, when he's not home, I straddle a chair, my head thrown back.

Now, Asad watches me as I come. A moment later he does, his hand tightening on my hair, pulling it back. I manage to lean forward, sink my teeth into the soft flesh of his shoulder. Afterward, he slumps against me as I try to peel the sounds of our breathing from any noise in the hall.

Once, someone nearly does walk in on us. As the kitchen door opens, I fly off Asad, who jerks down his shirt. When the boy comes in, he looks horrified to see us sitting there smoking, sipping the dregs of our tea.

"Henri! *Ça va?*" Asad calls. The boy hurries out, staring into his cereal bowl. "What's wrong with him?"

"Oh my God . . . " Asad's penis has popped out from beneath his shirt; it stands pink and erect against the table. We laugh and he grabs my hand, leaving it like that as we run for his room.

MY YOUNGEST AUNT on my mom's side lived in my grandfather's attic, along with her baby and her truck-driver husband. When they moved out, I wanted to go along with my father to help him clean up, but at thirteen, was deemed too young to witness such squalor. They had left behind mountains of trash: dirty plates, clothes, soiled diapers. My father and uncle spent the weekend hauling Hefty bags down the three flights of stairs, leaving the stuff least likely to attract maggots—old newspapers and magazines—for last. My mother ventured up there a few times, offering by way of assistance her disgust at the way her sister had lived. Sunday evening, however, she came into my room with a book.

"I shouldn't show you this," she said, handing it to me.

Headmaster Cockley's School for Wayward Trollops. On the cover was a teenage schoolgirl in an impossibly short skirt and a see-through blouse. She was sucking a lollipop. From the way she had positioned herself atop the desk, one could tell she would be a trying case for Headmaster Cockley.

"Whoa! Can I read this when you're done?"

"Are you crazy? This is no ordinary romance novel, you know." Since I'd been nine or ten, my mother had been giving me her old paperback romances to keep me quiet during long rides in the car. She calmed my father's protests by explaining that "the good parts" were always toward the middle of the book, and that I'd never get to them, since she gave me a different novel each time. Unbeknownst to her, when given the opportunity to read about throbbing manhoods and the dastardly rogues they were attached to, I could read very, *very* fast.

Clearly, *Headmaster Cockley* would cut to the chase. A glance at the first page before my mother snatched the book away revealed there wouldn't even be a chase. I believe the first line went something like, "There's a certain class of young lady that will simply put anything they are given straight into their mouths."

"Aw, c'mon, Ma, please!"

My mother turned away for a moment, considering the stuffed animals lined up on my dresser. "If I let you read this, do you swear not to say *anything* to Daddy?"

"Cross my heart."

"And you won't ask me to read any of the others?"

"There's *more?*"

I never kissed a boy, not once, in all four years of high school. The minute I thought one of my guy friends had started to "*like* me like me," I'd avoid him until the feeling had passed. I turned down every request to go to a boy's house so we could "hang out or whatever." Yeah, I knew what "whatever" was. It was Father's Day at the School for Wayward Trollops, where the students showed off their fellatio skills to their friends' dads. It was the seven-page "training" scene in the fourth novel I read, about the harem. It was whippings and enemas and German shepherds and a supper club where the men ate their meals off of naked wenches. Hanging out with my friends at the mall, I'd suddenly fall into a trance, watching the crowds, imagining everyone disrobing and falling to the floor of the food court in a giant pile of orgy.

I also stared at the couples at school: the ones who snuggled on the lawn or walked slowly hand in hand through the bustling hallways, as though there were no such thing as a late bell. I wondered what books they had read.

"Will I ever get a boyfriend?" I asked my mother every day.

"Of course you will." She never grew tired of answering this. "You're just a late bloomer, that's all. You'll find someone when you're ready."

I didn't have sex until I was twenty-one. I don't remember whether the lights were on or off. I kept my eyes shut the whole time.

WHEN YOU HAVE only 53¢, you need a job. I have free Internet now, on Asad's computer, but the job sites for English speakers contain ads that are weeks old, and the postings are generally more "job wanted" than "help wanted." Besides, they're all for baby-sitting. I'd be just another brown-skinned domestic trailing after someone else's pale, bright-futured offspring, perhaps pushing a stroller that had cost more than my father's last car. Other people's houses: leering family photographs and the heat never turned up high enough.

What I need is a position in a quiet office where the phone never rings, perhaps a little shop where no one ever comes in and I can be free to arrange the pretty things, stare off into space when I grow too tired. But even the listings I find on the expat websites require working papers. I could be a waitress, but I was hopeless at it even in New York, where I could understand everything. What do people scream at you in Paris when you spill soup in their laps? And even if I get an interview, I'll never be able to find the place amid all the grand and twisting rues. Plus, the job will be in Paris, which is an expensive commuter-train ride from Asad's dorm, not to mention the possibility of having to also take the Métro every day during the long, hopeless stretch between starting work and getting the first check. You know what I need? A job.

EVEN THOUGH ASAD keeps the heater on, the window closed, and his arms around me, sometimes I wake up in the middle of the night and feel the wind, the way it felt as I huddled at a bus stop at 3:00 AM or trudged along the Seine at dawn.

Well, that's over with now, I think, snuggling more deeply into Asad's arms. The wind howls in reply.

A KNOCK ON the door, a cheery *"Bonjour!"* When I open my eyes, Asad is sitting up in bed, his eyes wild.

"It's the cleaning lady!" he hisses. "If they find out you're here … *Un moment, s'il vous plaît."* We jump to our feet, heads whipping about the tiny room.

"I could hide under the bed," I whisper. "Does she vacuum under the bed?" He gives me a new look, stomps to the door. I slip back under

the blankets, listening to his smooth, charming French. He was studying all night, so tired, just went to sleep. Can she skip cleaning just this
one week?

After he closes the door, he stomps to the computer, not looking
at me. He sits very tall and rigid before the blank screen, waiting for it
to start.

"I have a friend," he says finally. "He is rich. He works at a bank.
Maybe you could live with him."

"Why would he let me live with him? I don't have any money for rent."

He turns to the window, to the leaves beginning to turn fiery at the
tips. "You wouldn't have to. He would give you money."

My hands slip under the covers, then into my left sock. Flaps of soft,
dead skin on the ball of my foot.

He whirls around quickly, as though I have protested. "You can't
stay here! You see what almost happened—I could be kicked out on the
streets! Do you understand?" He is standing over me now, his nostrils
flaring in and out.

"You want me to move in with some strange man I don't even know?"

"What else? You don't speak French. You have no papers. You have
no money. . . . "

"Just because I have no money doesn't mean I'm a whore."

He drops to his knees, ripping his shoes out from under the bed. I
could've hidden under there; we could've put something in front of me.

"I talked to him last night." He is shrugging into his coat. "I told
him about you. He would give you thirty euros a day. You could stay
with him. You could save." His voice drops on the last word. After he's

gone, I can hear the cleaning woman in the next room, over the groan of the vacuum; she sings.

I dream I'm in bed, clinging to his mattress being tossed about by the sea.

I awake on his lap, my face wet against his coat. He is rocking me back and forth. "Forgive me. I say stupid things. We'll work it out."

That evening, we are both studying our respective foreign languages, humming snatches from the CD playing in his computer. "C'mere." He buries his face against my breasts, rubbing his head back and forth. "Stressed. I think I need a massage."

"Thirty bucks," I tell him. He laughs, sits up to kiss me softly on the mouth. When he pulls away, his lids are heavy.

"I don't like bitches," he says.

Until I was sixteen, I believed that in the Middle Ages, there'd been such a thing as unicorns. I didn't believe they had flown, though; I wasn't stupid.

One night Asad goes to a party on campus. He comes back after an hour, breathing heavily. "I was rock 'n' roll dancing," he says proudly. When he's at the computer, his hair swirls up in the back in such a way as to make his head look square. Behind him on the bed, I trace it in the air with my finger: a perfect square. The hallways resound with laughter, the sounds of all-night study parties. His phone never rings; the cleaning lady is the only one who has ever knocked on his door. When he eats he hunches over the table, shoveling and slurping, as though if he takes too long, the food will get bored and walk away. Watching him, I reach over and pull some of the hair on his arm. Hard.

"Aie! What was that for?" He starts, yogurt clinging to his bottom lip. I don't know. I love him; he saved my life.

I FINALLY EMAIL everyone I know. This would be one of those good times to practice telling the truth, but I just can't. When most people say they don't have any money, they mean they have to stay out of malls for a while, put everything on plastic until their next paycheck, make it a Blockbuster night. I can't tell anyone I have less than a dollar to my name. That I spent the night in a hole. That I'm living with a guy who fucks me but no longer kisses me. The people I know don't live in that world. I feel they'd despise me, not just for living there myself, but for thrusting the knowledge of its existence upon them. A person would have to be a trained cryptologist to detect any hint of trouble in my bright, chirpy emails. I get chirpy emails back: *Can't believe you're in Paris. . . . You're so lucky. . . . I wish I was there too. . . .*

THERE ARE THREE of them—whom I know about, anyway. A girl from Toulouse whose emails he reads after midnight, chuckling silently while I emit luscious, tempting sighs from the bed. There's an Egyptian woman who follows her husband into Paris on business trips. And a girl named Antoinette who leaves breathless messages on his phone machine, in French, of course. "You didn't understand that, did you?" he inquires lazily after each one. I don't know where this girl lives, but she sounds perilously close.

He fucks me only in parentheses now. Never in bed, but in a chair after breakfast or up against the wall just as I've stepped from the shower.

He doesn't trace my bottom lip anymore or stare at me when he thinks I'm not looking or call me baby or call me anything. We're always in the same tiny room alone, so why would he, I ask myself. But it would be nice if once in a while he called me, waited for me to look up, rather than just start talking like it doesn't matter whether I hear him at all.

WHITE WOMEN. THEY were everywhere—at least, to hear my mother tell it, or scream it, rather—during the increasingly frequent fights she had with my father. White women were in the front seat of the car, stretched naked across my parents' bed. They propped their long legs up on the glass-topped coffee table, which surely they weren't allowed to do. We weren't even allowed to drink our juice on the coffee table, unless we used a coaster.

It rained the entire year I was five, inside our apartment, after my dad got laid off. Light but steady, the occasional clap of thunder when the bills came. One could almost forget there had ever been anything else but silent dinners and the staring-out-separate-windows people my parents had become.

Then my dad found a new job. He got two suits and man perfume and left the house every morning with very fast steps. My mother spent most of the days of her twenty-fifth year on the couch, watching soap operas: breathless affairs, hushed assignations planned over candlelit meals at which people left most of the yummy-looking food on their plates. She had long stopped leaving food on her plate, or ours either. During commercials, she would watch the Lego empires being constructed or the dolls being scolded and herded off to bed. Everything was moving, except for her and the clouds that hung thick and black beneath the ceiling.

No sooner had my father walked in, loosening his tie, than the clouds would burst, raining white women all around. My mother would grill him, making him report on the minutest minutiae of his day. He'd given $5 for an office baby-shower collection? Why, was it his baby? Martha in accounting had bought him coffee that morning? Did she suck his dick, too? Before he could take us to the park, my father had to stand a long time in the shower, washing the sweat of white whores away, and eventually, he could kiss only the top of my brother's and my heads, lest we smell the pussies of the typing pool on his breath.

One day, as I was creeping beneath my parents' bed, my mother burst into the room and threw herself upon it. The springs shrieked beneath her new weight; she was sobbing. "I want to die!" she wailed over and over again. "I just want to die."

Underneath the bed, I was burning with disappointment. I'd spent the whole day looking under furniture and through closets, combing every square inch of the house. I was certain if I found one of the white women my father kept hidden, and introduced myself as his daughter, she'd give me a piece of gum. I'd be careful not to tell her I wasn't allowed to have any until I was six.

I MET A man in Rome, an American named Jamie, in an English-language bookstore on Via Torino. We ended up laughing so hard at each other's travel stories that the shop owner suggested we adjourn to the café down the block, *per favore*.

Jamie was crisscrossing Europe, writing a guidebook of restaurant reviews from a gay man's perspective. He took me to dinner in trendy Trastevere, where he scrawled on a napkin, "The house red is as fruity and ripe as our server, Amadeo." He left soon after, but we've kept in touch.

> *Bonjour, mon petit chou,*
> *As luck would have it, I am heading towards très gay Paris myself. On Monday, I'm meeting a magazine editor. Tuesday, I'm catching up with old friends. I'm seeing my ex on Wednesday, so he can see how gorgeously tan I've gotten since Greece. My train leaves at four for Spain that afternoon, but if there's time, I'd love to see you. We'll have some escargots (I know you haven't tried them) at this place I know in the Marais. Hopefully, they'll be as firm and garlicky as Amadeo was my last night in Rome. (Went back to the restaurant later that night for desert. Tell you all about it....)*
> *Bisous...*

"I have a friend in Italy." I turn from the computer; face my lover. "He's coming to see me."

> *Hey gorgeous!*
> *Good news! The editor I met today has a job for me, covering some spots down by the Côte, so I'm going to have to cancel for Wednesday. But don't hate me; I'll be back late Friday night, and we will have all of Saturday to be Americans in Paris....*

Wednesday morning, I wake up to Asad's hand on my forehead. "You're warm." He hops up to get me an extra blanket, tucking it all around. He brings me breakfast in bed.

"I can tell when someone's getting sick, and it's going to be cold out today." He turns toward the window, as though the trees will confirm this. "I don't think you should go out."

He doesn't know, of course, that Jamie has pushed back our "date" to Saturday. By the time Asad gets home, we both agree that I am feeling much worse, and I get a two-day reprieve from French lessons and job hunting. He hums as he serves me my meals on a binder, puts his arm around me at night, just like he used to in the old days, last week. When he goes to kiss me on his way out Friday morning, I warn, "You'll get my germs."

He smiles. "They'll go right through me. I don't keep anything I don't want."

Okay, don't hate me.

I've met someone. His name is Ricardo, he was my transla-tor in the Côte. He's lithe, swarthy, and even more delicious than the crème brûlée we ended up feeding each other last night after a wine-soaked dinner. To make a long story short, we're on our way to his family's beach house in San Sebastian, so I won't be able to see you after all. (Ohh, I can't stand when you look at me like that!) But I promise I'll write you soon and fill you in on all the caliente details. Give me your address, I'll send you a seashell. . . .

"So, what are your plans for the day?" It's eight thirty Saturday morning. Asad is up, walking briskly around the room, throwing open the curtains, turning on the computer, stretching as if he were about to run a marathon.

"I'm going to meet Jamie in Paris."

He stops mid–leg bend. "What? I thought that was Wednesday."

I shrug. "He had to stay until Friday anyway, so he just decided to hang out one more day before he left." Asad is on his knees now, watching me as I rise languorously from the bed.

"He must really like you."

"Oh, we're just good friends." I look at myself in the bathroom mirror. Three days of bed rest have done wonders. From the bedroom, I can hear my lover doing crunches, his painful grunts.

At breakfast, I watch him pour granola into a bowl, then dump yogurt on top, spreading the latter with a spoon as evenly as if he were frosting a cake. We both admire his handiwork.

"It's pretty," I say.

He nods. "I'm going to fuck it." He giggles, and tea comes out of my nose. It's the last time we'll ever laugh together.

I hum as I dress, whistle while I put on makeup. It starts out being for his benefit, but then the excitement of the day catches up with me. I'm going out. I'm going to see something besides these four pasty walls and Asad's back at the computer. I almost forget I'm not going to meet an actual person. I've so longed for Asad and me to go somewhere, to have fun, even if we just wander the city streets. I know he's under a lot of stress, hiding me here, supporting us both. I know I'm only a burden. But just because I don't deserve happiness doesn't mean I don't need it.

"What's wrong?"

"This belt won't go any farther, but my pants are still loose. They fit just fine in Italy." Asad pushes away his book, beckoning me over. He pulls my belt as tight as it will go, then forces the pin between the weaving.

"That better?"

"Perfect. Thanks, babe." I go for my shoes but he pulls me to him, buries his face in my stomach.

"I'm so tired," he murmurs. I sink my fingers into his hair. We had post-cereal sex, and the ends are still damp.

He lets me go, and I sit on the bed to put on my shoes. Asad slumps back against his chair, his mouth open a long time before he speaks.

"What time do you think you'll be home?"

"Oh, I dunno, we might stop by a party at some friends' of his. I think he wants to see an art gallery—"

"Okay, okay," he cuts me off. "Then maybe you should stay with him. Or do whatever, I don't know. Because I'm meeting an old friend in the city myself, and. . . . " He laughs a little, or makes a sound like a laugh. "And I might not come home tonight."

All this morning, it's been on the tip of my tongue to say, "If this bothers you, I don't have to go." I could hear myself saying it. But I didn't.

We stare off into the same space. Then I grab my purse. "Okay, well, see you tomorrow!" All the way down the hall, I want to turn and run back. All the way to the bus, I want to turn and see him running after me.

Once I get on the train, I feel better. I'm doing the right thing. He's going to see how much he misses me. And how can he miss me unless I go away? But I'll be back. And this game will be over.

TELL ME SOMETHING GOOD BEFORE YOU GO

CH. 12

I spend the day at bookstores in the Latin Quarter, stop by gloomy Gare d'Austerlitz to check the departures for Spain, just in case Asad wants to know what time Jamie's train left. In the evening, I wander around the Marais, the stylish neighborhood near the Louvre where Jamie and I were to have had dinner. One day, Asad and I will be one of the couples leaning toward each other across a tiny table at a café. We'll pause in boutique windows and he'll press me against the wall on some cobbled side street, the ever-present rain falling lightly around us.

Around dawn, I sit on a bench by the Pont Neuf. Remind myself that this is the last night I'll spend on the streets, how it'll be easy from here on out. Then the bells of Notre Dame strike five times, and I think of how I'm thirty, how I have nothing to show for my life.

BEFORE I WENT to Columbia High, my education had been painfully gentle. Though I'd attended nursery school in the next town, my parents were unable to find a private elementary they could afford. I spent what would have been kindergarten and first grade at home, reading *MAD* magazine and making friendly ghosts out of toilet paper. At seven, I started second grade at a school an hour away, a place so progressive the students were allowed to design their own curriculum—a tricky proposition when you're too young to even spell the word "curriculum."

I didn't sit at a desk until I was nine, when I attended the first of two Catholic schools. There, the nuns emphasized the basics, but many of the kids inscribed their names in the same textbooks their parents had used twenty-plus years before. We could always get out of a science lecture by asking, "But Sister, why do we have to learn all this if *God* made everything?"

Then I turned fourteen and we moved to the suburbs. Suddenly, I found myself in a huge, top-ranked public high school, surrounded by kids who spoke in code: GPA, SAT, AP, homework. My schoolmates rushed from class to library to test-prep courses, bent double beneath the weight of their book bags. Before exams, Sunday afternoons would be taken up with something called "study parties." A misnomer, I thought, to call something a party when there was neither alcohol nor cake. Having done well on the school's entry test, I was placed in upper-level courses with kids who'd swallowed the necessity of college along with their organic soy baby formula. My family were all big John Belushi fans, and the only time I ever heard college mentioned was when my parents called to us from the living room, "Hey, kids! Come out here! *Animal House* is on!"

Why were all my new friends working so hard? I wondered. You didn't need to get into a good school to get a good job to make good money. All you needed to do was *believe* you could get what you wanted. After all, that was how we'd managed to move to the suburbs. I took an à la carte approach to my studies, signing up for only the subjects that interested me: foreign languages so I could travel, then art, creative writing, drama—fields of knowledge guaranteed to make one a killing in la-la land.

Despite my prudence, I began to suffer stress headaches from watching my classmates overwork. Staying home was never a problem; it had been determined long ago that my royal blood made me delicate. I spent many a high school day languishing in bed, watching TV, nibbling listlessly at a microwave burrito.

Right before the end of sophomore year, I went to a diner with some friends and listened to them go on breathlessly about the colleges they were going to visit, what application-padding activities they were about to embark on for the summer. It occurred to me that the only thing my family planned on doing during the nine weeks was going to see *Die Hard 2*.

When I got home, I found my parents seated at the dining room table with a stack of bills. My mother was tearing each envelope open with a rather preemptive quickness, as my father stirred his spoon around in his tea over and over and over again. When I cleared my throat, they looked up at me, squinting a bit, as though they weren't exactly sure who I was.

"Hey, guys," I asked them, "how much money is in my college fund?"

It was just like those synchronized swimmers you see in the Olympics. In unison, my parents' jaws dropped to the table. Then they both sat back in their chairs. Then they both leaned forward, each expelling a breath that scattered some of the envelopes off the table and onto the floor. I don't know who laughed first, but pretty soon they were in sync again, pounding the table, hooting to the ceiling, gasping for air like they were going to die. As I stood there watching them, my mother held out her arm and reached for me, as though to make amends, but, still convulsing with laughter, almost slipped off the table. My dad lurched forward and caught her. The last thing I saw before I turned and stomped out was the two of them roaring in each other's arms.

"Don't go, kiddo!" my dad called after me. "I'll check. Maybe we have a coupon for college."

I slammed my bedroom door. My head whipped about my messy room as I searched for my journal. No matter—I had a better idea.

"Dear Diary!" I yelled toward my door. "I've just been informed that I have no future!"

Even though their laughter grew louder, I wasn't mad. In fact, my heart was bouncing. It was the first time I'd ever seen my parents hold each other.

And the last time, for shortly after that, my dad moved to Sofa

City. One morning, after another of the marital scream-fests I'd grown to consider so much background noise, I found my dad asleep on the living-room couch. My mother started to banish him from their bedroom more and more—for making something she didn't like for dinner, for making one too many bad jokes at dinner, or for bringing home what was, according to her, the worst joke of all: his paycheck.

Soon he was on the couch every night. The entryway closet was cleared of coats and boots to make room for my father's possessions. He said he didn't mind, not at all. At a garage sale, he found a bureau that fit perfectly inside, still leaving him room to hang up his shirts. The toggle switch to the closet light broke, so he fashioned a new one out of a piece of thin rope. The rope came down almost to the floor. Rather than cut the bottom, he fashioned it into a noose.

When I questioned my mother about this, she said, "Do you think I would have kicked him out if I was getting anything out of having him in my bed?"

"But maybe he likes sleeping in a bed," I pointed out, an argument clearly too inane to merit a response.

Since we were now living in a well-to-do suburb, we received a lot of credit card offers. My mother always said yes. She redid her room, painting it in the most girlish shades of pink. Every surface was covered with lace, and the lace covered with Limoges boxes and other expensive trinkets. She got a hand-embroidered wastepaper basket for $80. We all got to know Rick, the UPS guy.

One afternoon, I watched as she opened a box and took out a trio of silk heart-shaped throw pillows. She had started to arrange them on her bed, when suddenly she sat down, clutching one of the hearts on her lap. "Did you ever think your life would turn out like this?"

"Um . . . I don't think it's turned out yet," I answered. Her head jerked up.

"Oh, shit! Did I say that out loud?" she asked.

"Wow," I quipped, backing out of the room, "you really know what to say to a girl to do her homework." I could hear her laughing as I walked down the hall. When I got to my room, I took my stuff out of my book bag and sat at my desk. I didn't do any homework. I just sat there.

IT'S HARD TO be special, especially when no one notices you are. This was the dilemma faced by my mother, Dana Elizabeth Thomas, née Wilson. She was called Bethie by her father, Dana Elizabeth by her mother.

"But the most important thing," my mother always told me, "was that for the first nineteen years of my life, not a goddamn person called me Mommy."

She grew up in Irvington, New Jersey, which, in the 1960s and early '70s, was a quiet, working-class town. The second of three girls and a boy, she was one of the town's few black students. She was pale, with thin, straight hair and angular features that were more striking than pretty; you would have had to look very closely at Dana to know that she was black at all. Not that many people were given the opportunity. Unlike her popular older sister, Dana had no use for after-school clubs, pep rallies, and dates with her classmates. "I didn't want too many friends," my mother would insist. "Popularity," she'd tell me, "is for losers."

Fresh out of high school in 1973, she took a job in the front office of a small company, waiting for life to begin. One of the few men working at the office was John Thomas. John was quiet and not terribly tall, but he had nice eyes, a neat little afro, and sideburns almost long enough to be daring. He was kind. She was bored. They went out.

On their first date, he took her to one of the matinees movie theaters used to have where you could see three karate movies for the price of one. At dinner, he winced when she ordered a piña colada, rather than the water he was enjoying.

"Whoa!" He held his hands up jokingly after she'd taken a big sip. "Slow down! Those things cost two bucks a pop."

"I think you're really nice, but I'm going to get back with my ex-boyfriend." Dana practiced saying this in the mirror that night after she returned home. Perhaps because there was no ex-boyfriend, she put off telling John while they dated exclusively for the next three months. Then she found she would have to tell him she was pregnant instead.

She didn't want to marry John. Even his name was boring. Dana had taken to calling herself Monique so people would think she was French. My future grandmothers were as different as two black women could be and, upon meeting, took an instant dislike to each other. My maternal grandmother had grey eyes and wore white gloves when shopping downtown, even in the '60s. My paternal grandmother had a houseful of children with different last names. A brief exchange of history revealed that Lady Mae, as my father's mother called herself, had worked as a cleaning woman for my mother's family years ago. She'd gotten fired after the necessity of catching three buses to get to the suburbs had caused her to be late one too many times.

"What in the world is a pretty girl like you doing with my son?" Lady Mae would ask my mother. She would go on to tell her that when he was a baby, my father was so ugly that Lady Mae sat him behind his two toddler sisters in the very back of the stroller.

"Besides," she'd add, "you're too light-skinned for him. You could get a man who's gonna have something." Perhaps Lady Mae was trying to discourage my mother because she sensed that if the younger woman ever had kids, she'd be direct competition for the coveted award: Worst. Mother. *Ever.*

But regarding her son's prospects, at least, she had a point. It wasn't so much John's past that turned Dana off, but his future—he didn't seem to have one. At thirty-two, he seemed perfectly content playing free gigs with a cover band, or pickup games of basketball at the local park. Shortly after they met, he was laid off from their office and barely supported himself with substitute-teaching jobs. His car always seemed to break down. What's more, even at eighteen, Dana knew she was destined for greatness. My father was too cheerful to be great.

"Tell me something good before you go," he'd singsong every night before they hung up the phone. No, even though John had gotten her with child, he would never do as the father.

"I'm pregnant, so I'm leaving for L.A. in a few days," Dana told my dad on what was to be their last date. While he sputtered, she explained that it was important to go to the West Coast. She wanted have her baby on the beach, like a hippie.

The next day, John put his car up for sale, gave up his apartment, and began to sell his belongings. He was coming with her. No baby of his was going to be born on the beach—sand had germs.

Los Angeles was the land of dreams, of movie stars, of Dana's favorite soap opera, *General Hospital,* whose opening credits, of course, showed L.A. General. There, a few days before Dana's nineteenth birthday, I had an uncomplicated and unhippielike birth. Surely in L.A., during Dana Elizabeth's strolls down Hollywood Boulevard, someone who was Someone would finally notice how special she was—even when tailed by a whistling, stroller-pushing, carless husband.

If she'd known how much fun it'd be to have a baby, she would have had one years earlier. John cooked for her, joked her out of her homesickness, got up at night with the kid. He found a good job and they moved into a complex near Hollywood, full of women not much older than she. The women were all models, actresses, or trying to be. They invited Dana to their beanbag-filled apartments, plied her with cheap wine and tales of auditions, affairs, adventures, all the while bouncing the baby on their knees.

"I can't wait to have one of these," they'd confide. "I'm going to settle down the minute I stop having fun."

She never should have had the baby. Sometimes she'd sit in the tiny apartment, listening to it gurgle happily in the infant seat until she wanted to scream, "Oh, shut the fuck up!" The kid started to crawl at five months and put everything in her mouth. After being slapped, she would have the audacity to scream for hours. If you're old enough to crawl, why wouldn't you understand the concept of dirt?

By the time the baby turned one, John's homecomings, which used to be reserved for Dana, now consisted of the baby's sprinting across the living room to him as though her life depended on it. He would take the kid for a walk, and Dana would hear them whispering before the front door closed behind them. When John returned with the little traitor in his arms, he would ask Dana, in a voice as close to disapproving as he could muster, "Did you and the baby get into a fight today?"

He didn't understand. Every day, a second after dawn, the baby would pull herself up in her crib and yell, "Ay, what we gonna do today?" She talked incessantly and never about anything of interest. She played with more than one toy at a time and threw a fit to be rescued from the nursery if she was still awake when Johnny Carson came on. She was never sleepy.

"You were like a nightmare I used to have as a little girl," my mother would tell me as I got older. "Where I'd put my Beddy-Bye doll down for the night and her eyes just wouldn't close." She would shudder, remembering. "I'd sing to the doll, I'd scream at her, I'd try to force her eyes closed with my hand . . . but no matter what I did, I just couldn't win."

THE NEXT MORNING, I ride the Métro for a while, but I'm too tired to sleep. At 10:00 AM, I call Asad with the phone card he's lent me and we meet at the bus stop in front of the dorms. I've bummed a piece of gum off some guy on the RER, in order to be minty fresh when Asad and I kiss.

We meet at the bus stop. I smile at him. He shakes my hand.

We start for the dorm, leaves crunching under our feet. "So, what did you do yesterday?" I ask.

"I met my friend. We went to a café. I was home by eleven." He watches my face. I clench it like a fist. "And you?"

All night, I've been picturing him with some... "Oh, about the same."

By the time I've taken a shower and gotten into bed, I feel better. Room sweet room. I awake at dusk to him nudging me, slipping off his shoes.

"Hmm?" I murmur.

"Can you get out of my bed? I want to sleep for an hour."

I sit at the desk and pull out my French book. Chapter 17, Subjunctive Tense: "If I were..." "If I could..."

In exactly an hour, he rises and rummages through his little refrigerator. I've eaten nothing since breakfast the day before. He stalks to the door, then pauses with his back to me. "I'm cooking dinner with some students who are fasting." (It's Ramadan.) Then he leaves.

In my notebook, I write him a long letter. The words spill off the page like rain. When he comes back, he immediately gets on the phone.

"Hey you... yeah, I just want to see how you are.... Okay, then, I'll see you next weekend. Can't wait. *Je t'aime.*" I love you. He goes back out.

I run to the cupboard and gulp down a candy bar, terrified he'll come in and catch me.

I'm in bed when he comes back. I've slipped the letter under his pillow. He turns on the computer, starts playing music I've never heard before. It sounds like a chorus of angels.

"Did you sleep with him?" he yells at the screen. I sit up in bed. He's rubbing his hands across his eyes, as though to erase them.

"No! I told you Jamie was taking the train to Barcelona that evening. He had his luggage with him. I dropped him off at eight thirty, and then I just walked around all night. That's what you wanted, isn't it?" We glare at each other while the angels sing. I slam myself back down against the pillow.

Good, now he feels guilty. My heart is pounding against the sheets. That was hell, so much worse than I thought. Love is hard, I decide.

Deep in the night, he turns over and throws his arm around my waist. I open my eyes, see the stars on the ceiling. *Thank you, God.* I weave my fingers through his. He wakes with a start, jerks his hand away. I lie unblinking in the darkness, until he starts to snore again. Then I slide the letter from beneath his pillow, stick it in my bag.

At dawn, I stare out the window at the trees; they don't make any sense. By nine I'm hunched over the desk with my French book, reading an essay about Claude's visit to the cheese shop. Asad sits up in bed, spends a long time watching me.

Finally, he rises to sit at the computer. He doesn't turn it on. With his back to me, he says my name. Finally.

"Yes?"

"When are you leaving?"

INTO THE WILD

CH. 13

"You ever hear of the Parc de Sceaux?" Asad asked once, pointing it out to me from the window of the bus. "It's beautiful. We'll go there sometime." I go there now, after we officially "break up" that afternoon in a nearby café. It's a long walk, but I carry only my knapsack. Asad has grudgingly allowed me to leave my large suitcase and duffel in his room. For a week at most, he tells me. Surely that's long enough to find somewhere to go.

He has no idea how little time I need. If there's anything my failed suicide attempts have taught me, it's the importance of playing to one's strengths. I should have known I would lack the temerity to jump from a high place, the patience to starve to death, the tolerance for the physical discomfort of anything more than a paper cut.

What I *can* handle is what I've coveted most desperately since I came to Paris: sleep. My new plan is to wait in the park until nightfall. After everyone leaves, I'll go somewhere secluded, slip off my jacket, and fall asleep. I'll freeze to death, just like in *How to Build a Fire,* by Jack London. True, the guy in that story had been in the Arctic or something. How cold would it have to be? I wonder. But I'm sure I'll start shivering when I stop walking. I'm buoyed by the fact that on the way over, I sneeze twice.

The Parc de Sceaux is manicured verdure: hedges formed into mazes, impossibly tall pines cut into perfect triangles.

I sit on a bench in front of a fountain where a walkway jets up from a square lake. People walk tiny dogs, jog. I savor the chill wind, the cold seeping through my body from the bench. I'm probably dying already.

Since first thing this morning, ever since Asad asked me when I'd be leaving, I feel as though I've spent my whole day doing some form of crying: weeping, wailing, sobbing. Sometimes, out of desperation, I've clapped my hand over my own mouth, my eyelids fluttering humming-bird-fast in an attempt to try to stop the tears that fall anyway.

Now, as I sit on the bench, growing numb from the cold, I find I'm equally numb inside. I feel light, clear, as though someone is holding a cool, steady hand upon my fevered brain. I may look like I'm staring serenely at the lake, but inside I'm fighting to hold on to the relative bliss of emptiness. It's hard to cling to nothing. Since my plan involves sleep, my mind starts to try to drag me back, to remember the last time I had a bed of my own, a door to close on the world, a place within it.

MY FIRST NIGHT with Donatella's family, we had dinner on their rooftop terrace. They lived in Cassia, an upscale neighborhood, far from the traffic and smog of central Rome. She and I and her husband, Bruno, made halting small talk across a table laden with platters of cheese and sausages, glistening olives. They apologized for their English, brightened when I told them, quite honestly, that theirs was far better than my Italian. They needed a tutor for English, they explained, because they felt the boys had no future without it. "We are simple people," they told me, as the moon shone down on their penthouse apartment, "but we want the world for our boys."

That first night, the kids were on their best behavior. Marco, the older one, was too shy to demonstrate the bit of English he was learning at his private school, but nodded when I asked if he would teach me a little soccer. Seppe, though only five, was not to be outdone. During a lull in the conversation, he stood up on his chair and serenaded us with the three English words he knew from TV: "Hello! Coca-Cola! Sexy!" A bottle of wine later, more hilarity ensued. When asked what my former boyfriend did for a living, I tried to say he was a lawyer, but instead of "*avocato,*" I said he was an avocado. Marco and Seppe fell off their chairs.

And the last night. Even after Donatella had turned on me, then turned me out onto the streets, I was too ashamed to say anything. I would have left quietly the next morning if, as he was giving me my final pay, Bruno hadn't sneered, "Americans . . . I should have known you'd be too lazy to work."

I retorted that his wife wanted me to help her cheat on her thesis, so I guessed she was American, too. I expected his eyes to widen. Instead, after staring at me for a moment, they slowly closed. Obviously, something like this had happened before. He went straight into the kitchen, where he must have confronted her, because the lady began to protest too much.

That night, after I booked my train, I packed slowly, with an ear for the knock at my door. Obviously, it would be impossible to stay. But I wanted Bruno to apologize, to admit that my having to leave wasn't my fault. There had to be something that wasn't my fault.

Instead of a knock on the door, there was a note taped to the outside of it. Could I please leave before seven, when the boys got up for school? To see me depart so suddenly, when they'd thought I'd be there all year ... it would just upset them, *capisce?*

At 6:30 AM, I was creeping out of the room with my bags. (My train to Florence didn't leave until two in the afternoon.) I almost tripped over Marco, huddled in the hall. He stood up, instantly awake. "You go now," he sighed, staring at my knees. When I nodded, he held out his hand; I held it, wondering if mine had ever been that soft. And all I could think of in the cab, on my way to catch a train to do God knew where with very little money, was how he'd probably waited since dawn just to say good-bye. And how maybe all the trouble he and his brother had given me was a way of coping with such crazy parents. Deep down, he was a good kid. I hoped the world would let him stay that way.

WHOA, I THINK. The fountain begins to blur a bit and I quickly blink back the tears. A mother's betrayal, a father who wouldn't stick up for me, getting kicked out of the only home I had. It was like my childhood, but condensed, with subtitles.

Maybe that's why I ended up in Paris. That's why I'm in this park now. Because I've had this terrible history. And it keeps repeating itself. And I don't know how to make it stop.

There are mosquitoes, or something like them, buzzing around my face. I slap them away. I don't know why I can't let them have a little blood; it's not like I'm going to need it. But I can't just sit there and take that.

Finally, the sky grows a deep blue. The joggers thin. The strollers turn into suits, walking swiftly toward home. When I haven't seen anyone for several minutes, I get up and walk through a tangle of trees, up a path where I've seen people being led by their dogs. Lucky dogs. I have to pee like I never have before, have had to since the café, where Asad officially ended a relationship that had existed only in my mind. But I hadn't wanted to let him out of my sight. I knew the moment I did, he would be gone.

The woods, on closer inspection, are surrounded by thin, wire fence, about chest-high. It's getting dark fast and I walk more quickly, searching out an opening. Finally, I find a spot where the fence has been stomped down. I step over the wine bottles and condom wrappers to a patch where some bushes will hide me.

Nature can be unappetizing up close. The soft grass is only a thin layer of green over the mud. Roots from the bushes push up from the ground like snakes. The mosquitoes have followed me.

I take off my coat and lie down in the pajama pants and tank top I slept in the night before. I hear scampering. Real close. I hug my arms to my chest for warmth. *Remember, you're supposed to be freezing to death.* I drop my arms. The sky above is thick with black birds cawing through the treetops.

I hear an owl. It's the first time I've ever heard a real owl. "Hoo," I whisper back. More scampering. I imagine that when I die, my bladder will immediately gush forth. Whoever finds me the next day will think I'm responsible for the wine bottles and the condoms. I think of tidying up a bit. I sneeze. More scampering, even closer. I open my eyes. The big birds have disappeared, replaced by smaller ones with rapid flapping movements, just like bats.

Bats. I'm on my feet, running. I turn around and run back to grab my coat. I turn around again and trip on a wine bottle, skidding into a pile of prickly bushes. I get up and run back again; I forgot my knapsack. I pick my way carefully over the wine bottles. I squat behind a massive tree, my pajama pants around my knees, and pee an ocean. It takes such a long time that while doing so, I manage to pull all the prickles out of my hands.

Back out in the park, night has taken the charm from the shadowy mazes and giant trees shaped like spears. Besides, anyone could be hiding in here, some homeless person. I could be killed. Racing toward the entrance, I find this would be impossible. When the park closes at night, they shut the gates, twelve feet high all around.

"*Excusez-moi.*" The perfectly round groundskeeper, coming out the side door of a little gatehouse, nearly drops his sack of garbage. He turns on his flashlight and peers at me. "Um *désolée. La parc est fermé et je suis . . . trappé?*"

The groundskeeper and his boss have a good chuckle, walking me to the employee gate. The park controllers patrol on horseback, and they show me the stables.

I must promise them I will be more careful. Am I enjoying Paris? Why, it's such a lovely night, why don't I go to the Eiffel Tower?

PART TWO

"The important thing is this: To be able at any moment to sacrifice what we are for what we could become."

—Belgian Naturalist
CHARLES DuBois

COS'È
LA
VITA

CH. 14

P aris does a fantastic night: the Parthenon and Sacré-Coeur in the
moonlight, golden domes and angels with swords thrust toward
the black sky. In the mornings, people really do carry fresh-baked
baguettes tucked under their arms and little old men do sport black berets. Hang around Notre Dame long enough, and street musicians will
start playing that sexy-sad French music on their accordions. There are
buildings so grand, I'm not sure people are allowed to walk by them, and
statues, statues everywhere, looking as if any minute they could leap off
their pedestals and strut down boulevards wider than any I've ever seen.
It's as if years ago, whoever built this place just knew it would be Paris.

WITH NO MONEY for the train, I follow the road signs for eight hours,
finding my way back to the city around 3:00 AM. I head straight for the

Seine, leaning over the wall to drink in the sight of the black, lapping water. It's the safest I've felt in days.

I'm wandering down Saint-Germain-des-Prés when I feel someone behind me. I turn and see greased hair, leather jacket, chubby face. I slow my step and make eye contact with the guy, waiting for him to look away, walk on. He doesn't. There's a darkness about him that stays before my eyes even as I turn away and pretend to study the shoes in a store window, to give him time to pass. He walks up to me, drapes his arm around my shoulder, whispers, "*Bonsoir.*"

"Hey ... hey, no," I say eloquently, backing away.

"You are American?" he asks in English. He pulls me close to him. "You want to come with me?"

I shake my head, shrugging him off. I look up and down the deserted streets. When I turn back, he's holding out some money.

"Here, here, for you. You want to come with me?" It's €30.

I back up to lean against the wall. If I stand still nowadays, my legs begin to shake. Suddenly, my way out becomes clear.

Just like my family and I found our way out of the inner city and into the suburbs, I can make that €30 last me forever. All I have to do is *believe* it will.

It's so easy, I want to laugh out loud, but the effort would hurt my empty stomach. How could I have forgotten all I've learned?

I will believe that with this money, I can afford to go to an online café and buy a really cheap plane ticket to New York. Believe I'll have enough of the €30 left over to get an apartment in Manhattan: hardwood floors, exposed brick, a fireplace that I'll keep burning all year round. With the rest of the money, I'll buy the biggest bed I can find and so much food I won't be able to close my refrigerator. And next door, right next door, will live the sweetest guy in the world. He'll tell me later he fell in love with me the minute he saw me. He'll say that first day, "Where have you been all my life?"

Of course, I'll have to do something in order to convince my mind that it already has the desired outcome.

I smile at the guy in the leather jacket. "Got a cigarette?"

IN MY FAMILY, we believed in a benevolent God. Benevolent, but not impartial. After all, didn't he love us the best? Weren't we smarter, wittier, and better looking than any family in the universe? True, it did rankle that we had been deprived of our royal birthright, that our vow of secrecy affected every aspect of our lives, even forcing us to wait in line with peasants at the snack bar in Kmart. Had they known we were nobility, surely the other shoppers would have fallen all over themselves to let us cut so we could get our Slurpees first.

But those indignities were more than compensated for by our secret knowledge of the world. Let all those other religions believe that their adherents were the Chosen People—it was really just the four of us. Only we knew that there weren't Ten, but only Three Commandments:

1) You can have anything you want, as long as you believe you can.

2) Don't worry about how to get what you want. Visualize it, and it will come.

3) *But,* you must do something to convince your mind that the desired object or outcome is already yours.

IN MY TWENTIES, I reread the books I had been raised on and found they contained advice on things my parents hadn't mentioned. Things like planning, saving, hard work. I guess those pages had been stuck together when they had read them. No matter, because the year I was fourteen, we put the Religion of Entitlement to the test.

Except for a brief stint in Florida, we had lived in and hated Newark, New Jersey, for as long as I could remember. Once I began eighth grade, however, loathing turned to fear. I was to start high school in the fall, and if private and parochial tuition in grade school had been prohibitive, the money for a comparable high school was out of the question.

"But," as my mother stated, "I would slit my children's throats before I sent them to public school in Newark, with that murderous bunch of pickaninnies."

"Dana," my dad mumbled, looking uncomfortable, "kids are just kids, wherever you go."

"Hey, Ma, whose throat would you slit first?" Stewie asked idly, without looking up from his comic.

"She would slit mine, stupid. I'm the one going to high school. Right, Mom?"

She didn't answer. All year round, the teenagers on our block shot off illegal fireworks. I looked up to see my mother at the window, watching them flash across the starless sky.

From that point on, we were on a mission. When we drove through good neighborhoods now, we weren't just along for the ride; we had to collectively imagine ourselves living there. Through the years, we had grown especially fond of the town of Maplewood, particularly the hilly and desirable area near the nature preserve. This despite the fact that there were very few apartments for rent and the houses all cost more than my dad made in a decade. Maplewood was beautiful—all sorts of grand and often historic homes vied for prominence beneath the ageless trees. These trees blossomed, grew verdant, and finally became wondrous shades of red and orange during the months of our search.

At the time, Columbia High School was one of the best in the state. We parked outside one afternoon in September. As the dismissal bell rang, my mother commented on how fresh-faced and wholesome the students looked.

"Where's the black kids?" I complained. "I'm sick of being the only black kid in my class."

"I see one, a guy with a blue book bag." Stewie pointed him out to me. "Hey! There's two guys with blue book bags."

"That's one kid," my father told him. "Put your glasses on."

"Besides, what does it matter?" my mother rebuked me. "I've told you a million times: You're not black; you're not white. You're simply *my children.*"

"Uh, we're both black, so that means technically the kids are, too," my dad pointed out.

"Well, I know you are," my mother sneered. "Drive."

In October, when I despaired of being a high school dropout without ever having gone, our believing finally paid off: We found an apartment that looked just like a house. It was the first floor of a two-family, across from a street with open gates at the entrance and homes that cost a bazillion dollars. Ridgewood Road—even our address sounded posh. Because we had believed, my mother told us, God had led us to our rightful place.

At ages twelve and fourteen, respectively, my brother and I finally had our own rooms. We could go outside whenever we wanted. That was when I began my habit of taking long walks up and down the steep, winding roads, breathing in the world that before had existed only outside the windows of our car. In bed at night, I would slip off my Walkman just to hear the sounds of no boom boxes, no firecrackers, or worse. In the morning, I would awaken to birds chirping in the trees. I hadn't known birds really sang to greet the day. I thought that was just something they made up for the movies.

I HAVEN'T EATEN anything but a candy bar in thirty-two hours; I've spent eight of those walking back to Paris. The cigarette the guy gives me blooms inside my empty gut like a mentholated rose. I grow dizzy and he puts his arm around my shoulder, steadying me.

We stop in front of a fancy building. "You live here? This is your apartment?" He seems put out by the surprise in my voice.

"I live here, yes. And my mother and brother." He smiles sheepishly. "And some other persons."

"I can't . . . we can't, then. Isn't your mother going to get mad?"

He speaks a little English, a little Italian, a little French. We mix our whispers in the three languages, squinting in the darkness as we work to translate and be understood. He tells me he's from Spain. I ask him if he speaks Spanish. "No."

"I just tell her you're my friend. We are talking only." He looks up at the building, not seeming to believe this will work. "Okay, no worry. We'll go to a bar I know. We'll get drunk, then *se niente importa.*"

In the Latin Quarter, our footsteps echo down the narrow streets. I hear American voices behind us, shouting, laughing drunkenly. I turn; maybe it's someone I know. His grip tightens on my arm.

"*Cazzo.*" Fuck. The bar he was telling me about is closed. We walk aimlessly down Rue des Écoles, past the Sorbonne.

"I wanted to go there," I tell him. "I always dreamed of coming here to study French."

"*Aspett',* I know a place." As we double back toward Saint-Germain, it starts to pour. We hail a cab. I melt into the back seat.

"*Combien?*" the guy, whose name I still don't know, asks the driver, a burly African with huge eyes.

"Eight euros."

"*Oh là là, mon amie.* I only have this." My companion holds out a handful of change, the biggest piece €2. The driver turns around and his eyes get bigger. They start arguing. Night surcharges. . . . But it is too much. . . . Well, take the bus. . . . Just take the money.

The driver pulls up to the curb with a screech. "Get out of my cab!" he yells in English. My date giggles and slides out.

"*Désolée,*" I apologize.

"Get out."

The rain follows us into Châtelet. We walk past the pedestrian mall–cum-*carnaval* where I went with Luciano. It's deserted, and I wonder where all those people with no place to go have gone.

He leads me down Rue Saint-Denis, a street full of massage parlors, sex shops, hookers. His hand comes up from my shoulder to caress my cheek as we walk. The women lining the streets wear high boots, short skirts. He ignores them like he knows them by name.

At the corner, he stops me. "Let me kiss you." He thrusts his tongue down my throat, licking all around my face like a frenzied Saint Bernard. When he lets me go, I'm gasping for breath. It's like being a little kid in the deep end of the pool at the Y, my kickboard suddenly slipping from my grasp. But not.

"Are you hungry? Do you want to eat?" Another kebab place: meat tumbling out of the sandwich, crispy fries. The can of Coke starts a tingling in me like music.

"You know," I say to him across the greasy table, "this is my first time. For money."

He looks away, shrugs. *"Cos'è la vita."* Such is life.

Back on the street, he takes out a key. He claims to know of another place but seems to have forgotten where it is, for he keeps trying, and failing, to open every apartment door we pass. I inquire politely as to what the *cazzo* he is doing.

"This is a master key. I paid forty euros for it." (*More than what I cost,* I think.) "It's supposed to open every door in the world." He passes it for inspection. "What do you think?"

"I think you should get your money back." He laughs and kisses me wetly on the cheek. He tries some more doors. Lucky number seven opens.

We go up a dark stairwell. Windows overlook a courtyard: bistro tables around a small pond, a tiny red bike, overturned.

We shake off the wet. "Where is this place we're going to when the rain stops?"

He spreads his hands. "Right here."

"Here? We can't stay here all night."

"Not all night. It don't take me all night." He starts to unbuckle his pants. I turn and look at the little red bike. In the center of the handlebars is a tin horn. I can almost hear it. When some little kid pounds on it, it would go, *Toot-toooot.*

"I'm not doing anything here."

"Oh, baby." He grabs me for a kiss, but this time I duck; I'm wet enough.

"*Ascolta,*" I hiss, "listen, let's just . . . " He wrenches my arm, whirling me around to face him.

"Come on," he says, yanking at my trench coat. He pulls my pajama pants down. I pull them back up.

"Wait a minute. I don't want . . . " He sticks his tongue down my throat again, his hands frenzied at my pants. I try to fight him off with one hand, the other holding up my waistband. It's no good; they're loose to begin with. Cold air on my ass.

"Stop!" I shove him in the stomach. He slaps me in the face. Bells chime in my ear. I feel his fingers hook in my underpants. I crouch down, working my pants back up with one hand, struggling to keep myself upright with the other. I know if I fall down, it's over.

He pulls my ponytail. A hairpin tinkles down the stairs. I almost topple back as he lets me go suddenly. I close my jacket around me, tying it tight. His penis jumps in front of my face.

"Listen . . . just wait. I don't want to . . . not here." He's grabbing my hair, trying to force my head toward his dick.

"Just wait . . . " I push at his legs, one hand still braced on the ground. He grabs me by my shoulders, starts slamming my head into his crotch. "Just suck it! Suck it!" he hisses.

I turn my face and hiss back, "*Aspett', aspett'!*" My cheek bounces off his penis like a rubber ball.

He lets out a growl and pushes me hard onto the floor. "What's wrong with you? Are you crazy?"

This time, he gets my pajamas and underwear off at the same time, tugging madly at the spot where my knees are buckled.

It's at this point that it hits me: *Hey, why am I whispering?*

I scream once, short but loud. He's on his feet in a flash. I hear voices, a rise of sleepy mumbles. We run down the stairs, pulling up our pants as we go.

Back in the storm, he sweeps me up in a gruff embrace. "You weren't very nice in there," he chides. The rain is like a fever—it won't let me have one slow thought. He is dragging me down a narrow side street, right by Pompidou. There's a woman lying under an awning, next to her shopping cart. She doesn't stir.

"It's okay, *bambina*, I'm not mad anymore. Let's go someplace else. I have the keys to a store where I used to work . . . "

"Listen!" I shove him away. "You're in this for sex, right? Well I'm in this for a nap. If we don't go somewhere with a bed, where I can get some sleep, then what's the point?"

He backs away from me so quickly that I turn around, bracing myself for a cop. There's nothing behind us but the night. When I turn back, his eyes glitter with tears.

"Fuck you, then!" he spits. "Fuck you!" He turns and disappears behind a curtain of rain.

Listening to the sound of his footsteps fade, I stand still; the world is shaking. I put my hands to my face, washing it with the rain. Then my arms beneath my jacket, the places on my stomach he punched. With my hand under my shirt, I can feel my heart. It's kicking and beating and alive. I become aware of the street lamp framing me in light, the roar of the wind, the rain pounding on the lids of trash cans like so much mad applause.

LIFESTYLES OF THE POOR AND UNKNOWN

CH. 15

A middle-aged couple enter a McDonald's on the Champs-Elysées. They scan the room over the heads of chattering teens and families hunched over their fries. There is an empty table with two soft drink cups and other debris left on a tray. The couple glance around, then set down their bags. Once seated, they become just two more customers and can linger over their drinks for hours.

I begin to see people like this everywhere. The men who have to be woken up when a night bus makes its last stop, the way they sway and doze where they stand as the bus pulls off, the ones who sit in Métro stations and don't look up when the train pulls in. I see pretty girls with dirty faces and old women who comb their hair, very carefully, in shop windows. It would be a lie to say my heart goes out to them. There is nothing in me but cold and the fight against becoming used to this. But they become real. It's like I've been struck with a second sight. Now, all around are these ghosts, doomed to wander in a world that looks right through them.

AFTER MY CLOSE call with the hypersensitive would-be rapist, I quickly learn to keep to bright, populated areas late at night. Couples in thick, matching sweaters kiss on street corners, clutches of girls trip out of cabs with their tiny purses and high heels. I walk by mile-long lines of glossy creatures outside clubs on the Champs-Elysées or the Bastille. These people love the night. They don't know it like I do: how the black sky flows into the black water, the way the wind chases you around the corner, the endlessness just before dawn.

Or maybe they do, and all that laughing and preening whenever I trudge by is just an attempt to break me.

I quickly learn to keep to the deserted, unlit streets at night.

IN THE PAST, when I wanted to be famous, I envisioned myself trashing hotel rooms with moody actor lovers before we left for glittering, celebrity-filled parties. When the paparazzi tried to photograph my love children, I would shield their faces, and whatever moody actor lover I happened to be with, who would be father to at least one of them, would smash the cameras to bits.

Once I decided to quit acting, however, I settled for just being great. At what, it hardly mattered. I wanted people to marvel at my brilliance, excuse my eccentricities, snap the odd photo of me looking piercingly off into the distance of some dark, smoky café.

But as the years went on, I would've traded that for not getting my lights shut off, not walking into the kitchen to see a roach as big as my foot, not hearing someone in the office on a Friday afternoon say, "Thank God it's Friday!" along with the accompanying murmurs of approbation, as though that person had just coined the phrase. My fondest dream then was to just be all alone, to not have to talk to anyone, to be able to walk around all day with no responsibilities, nothing holding me down.

Now, as I drift through the lovely, lonely streets, I wonder why, of all the lives I've wished for, this is the one I've gotten.

THE LAST THING my mother wanted was to be famous. "I couldn't imagine it," she'd say often. "Reporters, fans, the entire world up my ass." She'd say this whenever reading the *National Enquirer,* when we were standing in line for a movie, and especially when we gathered in the living room to watch *Lifestyles of the Rich and Famous.* One Sunday evening as the show was ending, as the vedy British host Robin Leach bade us champagne wishes and caviar dreams, I turned from my spot on the living-room rug and looked at my parents on the couch. My father was staring down at the pile of two-for-one coupons from the *Sunday Star-Ledger* he'd cut out on his lap. My mother was looking out the window, just like she did on sunny spring days when she wanted to go out for a walk, if only we didn't live in Newark.

"I have an idea! Let's make our own show." I suggested. "We'll call it *Lifestyles of the Poor and Unknown.*"

Filming was intense. As a family, we had to be photo-ready

whenever one of the four of us chose to narrate our seemingly quotidian but secretly fascinating doings.

"The Thomas family enjoys a light lunch at a five-star hotel on the Riviera!" As narrators, we quickly picked up the vocabulary used to describe the über-privileged. As subjects, we learned to freeze: heads tilted artlessly toward each other, so engrossed in conversation we momentarily forgot our plates of leftover tuna casserole.

"The fabulous Thomases caught in the midst of a shopping spree on Rodeo Drive!" We would all shield our faces from imaginary paparazzi, as well as actual bemused onlookers, as we dashed into the safety of Kmart.

"Movie star Dana Thomas goes bargain hunting in preparation for her next movie role as the wife of an office clerk." My mother loved that one. She flashed my creative father a dazzling smile as she looked up from a box of tattered romance novels at a garage sale. The woman selling them seemed to get into the spirit of things, too, by remaining frozen in her folding chair until we made our purchases and drove off.

The absolute best times for publicity, however, were when one of my father's cars broke down along the highway. These cars, which he always bought used and never for more than $200, made exits worthy of Kabuki. The engines would never deign to expire quickly. Instead, they would force the entire car to jerk back and forth, shake like a vibrating bed in a pay-by-the-hour motel, and emit moans of woolly smoke from underneath. If we were lucky, after my dad pulled over to the shoulder and lifted the hood, there'd be a small fire.

"Out! *Out!*" my mother would yell. My brother and I knew the drill:

1) Seatbelts off. (Usually, the car, made before we were born, wouldn't have them.)

2) Climb out the back-seat door of the side facing the shoulder of the highway.

3) Still remaining behind the shoulder's white line, take five giant steps sideways so that if the car blew up we wouldn't be hurt.

4) Be sure to remove all snacks, coloring books, etc., because if the car blew up, we wouldn't be able to go back and get them.

"The famous Thomas children wait for their limo to stop being on fire." I'd nudge Stewie. "Meanwhile, they take some time to greet their fans." Standing by a smoking heap of metal on the shoulder of the New Jersey Turnpike, my brother and I would smile and wave to the passing cars, most of whom would smile and wave back with equal enthusiasm but without, in my opinion, our regality.

"What the *fuck?* What are you doing?" My mother would pull us back toward the car, which would still be barfing smoke to the sky. "Are you two crazy?"

Not crazy. Just famous. Sometimes it's hard to tell the difference.

THOUGH MY MOTHER constantly assured us she wouldn't want to be famous, it was an unassailable fact that one day I would be.

"Everyone says you look just like me," my mother pointed out, "and God knows I'm gorgeous." Plus, I was talented—hadn't I taught myself to play the theme song to *Rocky* on the Magical Musical Thing? I made my parents spit up their Hawaiian Punch every night over dinner with my imitations.

DAD: "Honest, hon, I didn't lose my job—I know exactly where it is."

MOM: "Who says you can't put butter on french fries? They're the same thing as mashed potatoes. . . . John, do you think I look fat in these jeans?"

I HAD MY first audition at seven. My mom called me into the living room and pointed to whatever came on TV: "Can you do that?" I could do anything. I could sing the Oscar Mayer song with my legs swinging over the arm of the couch, so I looked like that little boy perched in his wagon. I jumped up and down in open-mouthed glee when Ed Mc-Mahon rang my doorbell and handed me a gigantic check. I pointed to the sky and lisped, "Bosth, Bosth, de plane, de plane!"

"Good. That's really good," my mother murmured, her eyes flicking back to the TV, as though for confirmation. "You know you can be anything you want to, right, sweetheart? You know you can be a glamorous movie . . . get your *fucking* finger out of your nose! You know you can be a movie star, don't you?"

I shrugged distractedly, deep in thought. What was I supposed to do? After all, my nose wouldn't just pick itself.

"You don't want to be a loser like your father, do you? Working like a dog and not making any money?" my mother continued. "You don't want to be like me, stuck in a tiny apartment all day with no one to talk to but a couple of kids."

I shook my head so vigorously, the barrettes on my pigtails almost blinded me. "I'm going to get famous when I grow up, Ma.

And buy you a big house. . . . " My mother swept me up into a hug. "And," I added, my voice muffled into her shoulder, "I'll buy you some friends to talk to."

I almost got whiplash, she held me away from her so fast. My eyes were wide and innocent—just like the little boy's on the Oscar Mayer commercial, just like the midget's on *Fantasy Island.*

After a moment of studying me, my mother said, "All right, that's enough for now. Go back and play." Every once in a while, I'd look up from my jigsaw puzzle to see her eyes trained on me. The director never called, "Cut."

ONE NIGHT, DURING the wee hours, I take out my ATM card and try to make a withdrawal. I've been more than €400 overdrawn since Italy, but I keep thinking maybe the bank will forget. As I type in my PIN code, I think of a big plate of food, placed piping hot before me, of stretching out beneath a comforter on a cloudlike hotel bed, a flight back to New York. . . .

After the machine rejects my card, sticking it back out like a tongue, I linger for a moment, swaying and shivering in the warmth of the vestibule. I almost wish someone would sneak up behind me, stick a gun in my back, demand all my money. I'd probably fall on the ground laughing if they did. I'd probably laugh until I died.

THE NEXT MORNING, I'm gassy. It enrages me. I haven't eaten properly in days. What the hell am I farting from?

LATELY, IF I see a new-looking cigarette box on the ground, I kick it to make sure it's empty. Even when I'm beyond hunger, have ceased to think of the spitlessness of my mouth, the need for cigarettes never leaves. I've always smoked mine right to the butt, but am now noticing not everyone does. I begin to see cigarettes abandoned after what looks like one, two puffs. Interesting. One night, I find one by the Seine. Look both ways, pick it up, and light it. It doesn't taste like germs. Dirty cigs, I call them. It doesn't take me long to learn the best spots to find dirties—right outside places people can't smoke: Métro stations, shops, schools. It's better than bumming cigarettes, more independent. I can take care of myself.

Wandering across the Pont Neuf during a predawn storm, I hear an animal whimper. My heart leaps as I scan the wet bridge. A puppy—scared, hurt maybe. A warm ball of fur I can cradle in my arms; I'll take care of it. I walk faster, head turning left to right, shielding my eyes from the rain as the whimpering grows louder. I'm at the end of the bridge before I realize the sound is coming from me.

COULD YOU PASS THE GREY POUPON?

CH. 16

"I don't have to look up my family tree,
I already know I'm the sap."—FRED ALLEN

B eing a failure is more than a job—it's a calling. Definitely not
for clockwatchers. For one thing, there's no easy way to mark
the passage of time. Even Hallmark cards aren't very helpful.
Oh, sure, there's:

CONGRATULATIONS, GRADUATE!
HAPPY HOUSEWARMING!
YOU'RE GETTING MARRIED!

But for me to make sense of my twenties, the sentiments would've had
to be more like:

You've Dropped Out of College! Here's Your Name Tag!

Great Audition! You Said Your Lines
Faster Than Anyone Else ... Next!

Happy Eviction! From 1-800-U-HAUL

You Can't Hold Down a Job,
but Way to Hold That Liquor!

And, last but not least:

That Frog You Kissed Didn't Turn into a Prince?
Oh Well, Fuck Him Anyway!

It was all my fault, of course. Young, brash, and just a few years out
of high school, I came home one day with my first bottle of perfume.
A saleswoman had Maced me in the face with it at Bloomie's, and I'd
fallen in love. In the past, I'd always used the same drugstore scent my
mother favored. Now, one whiff of my new perfume, and she became
convinced I was competing with her—as a woman or as a spokes-
person for Elizabeth Arden, I wasn't sure. She told me that she didn't
want my scent in the house. I could wait to put the perfume on until I
got out onto the front porch, or I could walk out onto the front porch
and keep walking.

I moved in with my best friend and her family, across town. A week later, they drove me to my parents' house to help me get my bed and other furniture. I walked into my bedroom to find it nearly empty—my stuff had been thrown out or stuck in the basement. My father confessed he slept in the room on an AeroBed he blew up every night. He looked ashamed when he told me, but I couldn't blame him. At that point, it had been about seven years since my mother had kicked him out of the bedroom. Imagine all those years not having a door to close, a space to call your own. It must've been like being homeless.

Once I started moving, it was hard to stop. From the home of my best friend's large, crazy, wonderful Palestinian family, I moved to an apartment in SoHo that I adored, until my credit cards fainted from the pressure of paying the rent, and then to a condo by Prospect Park in Brooklyn with my then-boyfriend, his old theater friend, and her interracial sperm-bank baby. I rented tiny rooms in tiny apartments and the waterlogged basements of houses. I crashed on living-room couches and office chairs, the top and bottom halves of bunk beds. Once, in a sublet in Queens, I accidentally watered the guy's plants with vodka. (Absolut horror!)

Part of the problem was that I never had any money, probably because I never had a job. Not for long. I tried my hand at retail, bakeries, waitressing—any job that required nothing more than the ability to simultaneously roll one's eyes while asking, "May I help you?"

But I'd so wanted more. I attended acting schools and acting classes and acting studios. I did plays where every night the cast was bigger than the audience. I did extra work in movies in which I had to spring to action whenever the director called, "Background!" (Just for the record, there's nothing better for an actor's ego than being lumped in with cardboard trees and the stuff that comes out of the smoke machine.)

One of the bigger roles I had was in children's theater. I played a neurotic chicken. My chicken was unable to convince Humpty Dumpty et al. that the fucking sky was indeed falling. I also couldn't stop the kids in the first rows from hopping up onstage and yanking the feathers off my costume.

"Now wait a minute!" I held up my wings only once, to stop a grown man who approached, eying my tail.

"I'm sorry. I just want to get a feather for my little girl." The man pointed out a child with her leg in a cast. "She can't get one herself, like the other kids, and it's not fair."

"Listen, mister." I stood up straight and smoothed what was left of my plumage. "Don't talk to me about fair."

SOMETIMES, OUT OF sheer desperation, homesickness, or both, I would move back in with Mom and Dad.

About a year after I'd gotten kicked out, my parents and Stewie had moved to the Jersey Shore. Had I gone back home when they were in our old house, my father would've gladly given me my old bedroom. This new house had only two, though, so I slept in the living room and my mother grudgingly let Dad back into the bedroom with her. However, she'd gotten furniture from Domain and didn't want me denting her new plush couches with my hapless body, so the weeks or months I stayed with them, I'd sleep on a comforter spread out on the floor. Each morning, I would fold the comforter and stick it into a closet, along with whatever suitcase I was currently living out of. Even my toothbrush I kept wrapped up out of sight. The years of living everywhere but my own home had taught me the wisdom of taking up as little space as possible. That when I left a room, no one should be able to tell I had been there at all.

One night, I was reading on the comforter before going to bed. I looked up to see my mother standing over me, shaking her head.

"You were so smart when you were little. You could've been anything." She sighed. "What the hell happened to you?"

"I'm not telling." I smiled up at her. "It's a secret."

I waited until her bedroom door slammed shut before I got up to turn out the light. When I lay back down on the floor, I curled up into a little ball, floating in a darkness I wished would never end.

ABOUT A YEAR before I left for Europe, everything had settled down, mostly because I had stopped: stopped auditioning and practicing monologues in the mirror and my Oscar speech in the bathtub. I had stopped going to therapy to figure out how to talk to my parents. There was no more need; I'd stopped talking to my parents altogether. I had moved from my beloved New York back to Jersey, to an unpretty working-class town where the neighbors left me alone in Polish, Spanish, and Russian. I commuted into the city by bus to a series of office temp assignments. These jobs required me to sit at a desk as the assistant to an assistant, some girl who would crack her gum in my direction while she said things like, "But you're not in school! Why are ya reading a book if you're not in school?"

The jobs paid me barely enough to survive, but it didn't matter, because I had learned the secret. My parents and their New Agey books had been wrong: The secret to getting what you want wasn't to believe. It was to not want anything at all.

I also stopped saying my prayers, for the first time since childhood. I still got on my knees every night before bed. But once I was down there, all I could do was stare at my knotted hands.

THAT JUNE, A month before I was to leave, my uncle Tommy invited me to lunch. It'd now been almost a year since I had spoken to or seen my parents. I assumed the two of them had been able to make excuses for my absence over Thanksgiving and Christmas; maybe they'd chalked it up to a little spat and everyone had believed them. People like to believe stories that don't require them to think. In the past, I had gotten fed up and gone months without speaking to my folks. On the first week of November, however, like clockwork, they'd start the appeasement process. They would phone me with promises of more understanding, less fighting, my Dad's Hot Dog Cheddar Surprise. It was important that we present a united front during the holidays, when those in the extended family would be around.

This time, however, they had pushed it too far and they knew it. At first, I'd been letting my phone ring when caller ID warned me it was them; then I changed my number altogether. Neither of them could use a computer—my parents thought the Internet was "evil"—so they couldn't get in touch with me that way, either. My mother's fiftieth birthday celebration had taken place during the second week of May. When I hadn't shown up for that, I guess someone in the ranks had decided to call in reinforcements.

My uncle Tommy, even in his forties, was like a big kid. It was about five years after VCRs came out that we actually got one (my parents thought recording TV shows to watch at a later time was "evil," too). So, for a while, I depended on Uncle Tommy to tape music videos for me at his house. Even when I insisted on playing George Michael's "Father Figure" seven times in a row, he'd never complained, only sighed and buried himself in a comic book. Clearly, if I wasn't talking to my parents, then someone needed to talk some sense into me, I guess the reasoning had gone, and I owed Tommy one.

I had to be careful. My grandfather and his second wife, who he'd married after becoming a widower; my aunts and cousins; and Uncle Tommy were the only family I had left, outside of Stewie, and I didn't want to lose them. But I was going to make it very clear to my mother's brother, and the rest of the family, that this break wasn't temporary. And it wasn't my fault. I could recount a million incidents, but I was certain the last one would do the trick.

THE LAST TIME I had seen my parents had been for my dad's birthday the year before. Earlier that week, I had called my mom to ask about the train schedule to their house. She'd asked me if I'd gotten him anything yet.

"*Have* I!" I exclaimed. Whenever I got around my parents, I felt like a kid again, right down to the need to speak in italics.

I went on to tell her that I'd found a company that specialized in old-fashioned candy. They made gift baskets according to the decade requested, including the '40s, when my dad had grown up. I felt this was the perfect gift for a man who could never see the price of a candy bar without telling us how he used to be able to get a veritable bucket full of Mary Janes for a nickel, like anyone wanted to eat that shit anyway. It annoyed me growing up, until I realized how rarely my father spoke of his childhood. Occasionally, he'd mention a teacher who'd encouraged his interest in drawing, the street games he and his friends had played, the funny characters who'd lived in his neighborhood. But of his family, he never spoke. He had at least four siblings that I remember, probably more, a mother, a stepfather. But after my mother told him we'd no longer be joining him on his biannual visits to his family, because they weren't "our kind of people," he stopped going, too. It was as if they had never existed. But candy did. It turned him into a little boy again. If you got him a 3 Musketeers or a box of chocolate-covered cherries, he'd open it right where he stood.

"He's going to be so excited," I told my mother. "What are you going to get him this time, or is he still using the nothing you bought him last year?"

"Ha ha," my mother said. "We'll see."

Since his actual birthday was a few days before I was set to visit, I called him the evening of. He sounded just as excited as I had a few days before.

"Guess what? Mommy got me a present," my sixty-one-year-old father said, referring to his wife. "She ordered me a whole gift box from this company that has candy from the old days. I don't even know how she found out about it. . . . "

As he spoke, I took the cordless phone into the dining room of my apartment, where the candy I'd ordered for my dad had just arrived. In its collectible tin. He wanted to name every type of candy he had received. I said please do, and describe it, just in case I wouldn't recognize it.

As he did, I played a game with myself: I picked up different pieces of candy and tried to guess what order he'd name them in: Zagnuts, Bazooka, Lemonheads, Brach's Root Beer Barrels. If I guessed right, I'd reward myself by hurling the piece of candy as hard as I could against the wall. If I guessed wrong, I'd hurl it as hard as I could against the wall.

"Whoa," he said a few days later. We were all sitting at the kitchen table at the house in South Jersey. My dad had just started to unwrap my present to him, but when he saw Maria Callas's face, he stopped. The smug smile my mother had worn faded as she tried to hoist her weight up off the chair, craning to see.

"What? What is it?" She glanced at me, too slow to hide the panic in her eyes.

I'd gotten him a box set of all of Maria Callas's songs. It'd cost a lot of money—enough for fifteen thousand buckets of Mary Janes, at least.

"You can have that present on one condition." I told him. "You don't make me listen to that crap with you."

"Get in here, punk!" my father called over his shoulder as he bounded for the garage, a room that was never opened from the outside, and in whose unheated space he spent weekends and evenings when bidden to leave my mother's sight. In the garage, he kept an easy chair, my old stereo. In warmer weather, he added a few houseplants that didn't require much light.

"Just a second!" I yelled after him. I turned to my mother. She'd been tracing patterns into the fake wood of the kitchen table. When she realized we were alone, her eyes got bigger. She still didn't look at me but kept her head down, one hand stroking her arm over and over again.

"That went well, don't ya think?" I drawled. "Funny, I was thinking of getting him candy just like you did, but I figured why buy him a present he's just going to shit out the next day?" She flinched but said nothing.

Dinner that evening was peaceful. Afterward, my mother and I chuckled to the evening sitcoms whenever the laugh track deemed it appropriate. My dad washed the dishes; snatches of "O Mio Babbino Caro" rose above the clatter in the sink.

Everything was fine until he and I were putting on our shoes by the front door so he could give me a lift back home.

"That really was good thinking, honey," my mother said sweetly, handing me my jacket. "Daddy's birthday present. I mean, what better gift can you buy for a faggot than opera?"

I didn't realize I shouldn't look at my father until I was already looking at him. He was tying his left shoe; his face was a void.

"You're right," I told my mother. "But you know, if I was a guy and I'd spent thirty years of my life with you coming at me in a muumuu, I'd be fucking gay, too."

"You have to try and understand Mommy," my father said as we pulled onto the Jersey Turnpike. "She's had a hard life." When I turned from the window to look at him but didn't respond, he added, "What are you thinking?"

"That maybe you *are* a faggot."

"Listen, kiddo. I know things aren't always easy around here. But we're a special family—"

"As in Special Olympics, you mean."

"If I tell you something," he began after a few minutes, "will you promise not to tell anyone?" I shrugged.

He told me that his mother had always hated him. Once, when he was three, he'd been scared by a loud sound in the street. When he'd gone running to his mother for comfort, she'd beaten him until he couldn't stand up. That was when he had decided he would never cry again. He told me this story as if he were Aesop, dropping some badly needed wisdom on me. "And do you know why she hated me?"

"Because she hated whoever your father was?"

"I didn't have a father."

"I know, but I mean, the guy who . . . you know."

"I mean, kiddo, that I didn't have a father at all. My mother told me over and over again that she wasn't sleeping with anyone when she got pregnant with me. I'm an immaculate conception."

He went on to tell me the story, of which I barely heard a word. What's the point of listening to the story of an immaculate conception? You know in advance it's not going to contain any sex.

When he had dropped me off, I headed for my bedroom. My legs felt so weak, I didn't even make it to the bed but collapsed right on the floor. Fortunately, my diary was on the floor, too, like most of my possessions. If only I could just clean my room, get it together. . . .

Dear Journal,

What the fuck is wrong with my parents?

I crossed it out. I wrote it again.

"DID YOU KNOW your great-grandfather Watt was a gardener?" At the diner, Uncle Tommy was pointing a mozzarella stick at me. Things were worse than I thought.

"*Why are your breaking your poor mother's heart?*" I expected him to rage at me. Instead of confronting me directly, however, he seemed to be intent on prodding me with every branch of our family tree he could think of. I had a relative who'd been a political activist for something stupid. Another who'd cut a 45 of one of his recordings and never sold any. By the time our hamburgers arrived, I was wondering how it was possible that my family had been boring for so many generations, that nothing had ever...

"Wait a minute! What about Grandma?" I asked Tommy, referring to his mother. "I want to hear about her and her parents. Whatever happened to the French girl? What kind of royalty was she? What about the soldier? Did he go back to America? Did he try to look for Grandma? Did he try to look for the French girl? What was her name, anyway? Mom would never tell us. And she told us never to ask Grandma, or any of you, because it was too upsetting. But I don't care if she gets mad now. I just want to know."

In our family, table manners reigned supreme. You kept your elbows off the table, kept your napkin in your lap, and never, ever spoke with your mouth full. Uncle Tommy's mouth was full of diner burger at the moment, so he couldn't answer my flurry of questions. But his eyes got very, very, very wide. So much so that I turned away and fixed my eyes on the condiments set on the table: salt and pepper, ketchup and mustard.

Mustard. Dijon mustard. Dijon—the town my mother had told Stewie and me our grandmother's family was from. Suddenly I realized that outside of Paris, Dijon was probably the only city in France my mother had ever heard of.

That was why we were never allowed to ask anyone else about my grandmother's parents. That was why no one else in the family had ever mentioned them. Not even during hushed send-the-kids-to-the-other-room conversations. My mother had made it all up. Whatever the true story of my grandmother's parentage was, I bet it was just as boring as everything else.

I was right. After he'd swallowed, Uncle Tommy told me my grandma's parents had been a pair of unmarried, interracial high-school kids. She'd been given up immediately for adoption. Grandma didn't talk about it much, but he thought he remembered her saying that her biological parents had been from outside Philadelphia.

Philadelphia, France? I wanted to ask. I knew it was no use.

"Where'd you get the idea that Grandma was French royalty?" my uncle smirked, though not unkindly.

After all that, I hesitated before ratting my mother out. *After all that.*

"From your sister," I said finally.

His mouth snapped shut. I looked down at my plate and gaily

dipped a mozzarella stick in marinara, struggling not to hum as I chewed. I wanted to give Uncle Tommy's rage time to simmer, boil over. Not just at his sister's having lied to her children, but at this blatant betrayal of their own mother's history. Ooh, wouldn't Grandpa be mad when he found out? Wouldn't my aunts finally get their revenge! My mother had always tut-tutted their child-rearing methods because they had worked outside the home rather than nurturing their children full-time. Like she had.

I didn't really want my mother's family to turn against her. Okay, maybe a little. But what I wanted more was for them to understand me, to know what it had been like to grow up with their daughter, or sister. Maybe they could provide a little insight into why she was like this. Or maybe someone could just reassure me that it wasn't my fault. I wasn't quite sure, you know?

I planned to wait until I saw smoke coming out of Tommy's ears. Then I'd tell him what had happened on my dad's birthday.

"Let me ask you something." I looked up. My uncle was smiling at me.

He continued, "Are you going to see *Spider-Man 2?* I had my doubts about the first movie, but it was so good, I really can't wait for the sequel." He was stuffing french fries into his mouth, faster and faster, as he spoke. "I guess it's not such a big surprise, though. You can do anything when you start with a good story...."

When I got home, I called Stewie. Stewie, who had morphed from a dorky little brother into the coolest guy on the planet, all the while remaining just who he was.

"Hey, sis!" he said when he answered. That's what he'd called me since we were kids. Far kinder than my former nickname for him: Birth Defect.

When I heard his voice, I knew I couldn't tell my little brother that we weren't royalty. Only I was aware of how much thoughts of our lost family affected his doings and loves. Stewie immersed himself in medieval fantasy books and for a while had tried to teach himself French. He'd cultivated a love (from afar) of expensive, hand-woven tapestries, the kind that hung on castle walls. He'd considered school even more of an eye-roll than I had; there was only one homework assignment I could remember his ever completing. It was an essay on an ancestor. He'd chosen to write about our hot-blooded, blue-blooded great-grandmother. I saved the essay for years. It began something like:

> *Once upon a time in France, there was a tiny French village where many French families lived. There was one girl who was the most beautiful. She was French, too...*

He and I never talked about it anymore—the possibility of a family with its own crest and a romantic history, who ate bread that didn't come presliced—but it was always there, in the background: Who We Could Have Been as a palliative for what we were fast losing hope of ever being. At twenty-seven, my brother worked as a bellboy. I was a backup receptionist, which is sort of like being a backup windmill. This had to stop.

"Grandma wasn't descended from royalty. Her parents were two teenagers with jungle fever from Philadelphia. Christ, not even. *Outside* Philadelphia."

I relayed to him exactly what Tommy had told me, as well as our uncle's complete befuddlement at the royalty story.

"Dijon!" I exploded at the sound of my brother's silence on the other line. "Just like the mustard. How stupid could we be? I guess we're just lucky she didn't tell us we were descended from a bunch of German aristocrats named Heinz. Aren't you going to say anything?"

"Who . . . me?" my brother whispered.

"Hold on." I reached for my pack of cigarettes on the kitchen table, only to realize I already had a lit one in my mouth.

"Listen, I'm not trying to turn you against her. But don't you think this whole thing's just a little, I don't know, *fucked up?* She's been feeding us this story for more than twenty years! And every time we messed up at work or school or just couldn't deal with some little, everyday thing, she would tell us not to worry—we were delicate or sensitive because of our royal blood. Well, we're not delicate, Stew, and we're not special. We're just like . . . I don't know, from New Jersey."

There was a long pause. All I could hear was Stewie exhale. My happy, hyper, perpetually unjaded little brother. It was the first time I had ever heard him sigh.

"Maybe she didn't make up that story to hurt us," he said finally. "Maybe she just wanted to give us something to be proud of." His voice had so much dignity at that moment. He sounded almost princely.

I couldn't blame Stewie for his reaction. Or Uncle Tommy. Not everyone was cut out for confrontations, estrangements, a Christmas alone in bed with no eggnog but a lot of rum. Losing your family is like losing your home in a land of continual rain. Everything you have becomes worthless. Everything you do is all wet. You might as well give up, go away, start anew in a far-off land.

CLOSE
YOUR EYES
AND THINK
OF ENGLAND

CH. 17

For better or for worse, the English language has taken over the world, and the corresponding section of the library at Georges Pompidou is lavish in its accommodations for students who need to become proficient. All the big shots are there: Edith Wharton and e. e. cummings, Tolstoy and Toni Morrison. On my third day back in Paris, I find a collection of Truman Capote's short stories. I carry it across the floor, past long tables and bent heads. I find a seat by the window and turn to *A Christmas Memory*. In moments, I can smell the fruitcake baking, the bite of fresh-cut Christmas trees. If I close my eyes, I can see the kites chasing through the sky.

Outside the large windows by my table, the rain has made the courtyard glisten in the dusk. As the month of October, and my homelessness, have worn on, I've become aware of a rough sort of beauty to my days, as though I am living in a grainy sepia film. Earlier this morning, I found two unopened jars of mousse, chocolate and lemon, abandoned on a stone bench. Having eaten nothing the whole day before, I felt my stomach contract with joy as I hurried over and slipped them into the pocket of my trench. Only then did I think to look around. There was a worker nearby, loading a truck. He was staring at me in mild confusion, the kind that turns into pity if you don't walk away fast enough. I snagged a plastic spork at a nearby KFC, too excited about the mousse to be depressed that there's a KFC in Paris. I took the mousse back to Pompidou, enjoying the velvety chocolate one in a large, self-contained handicapped stall. I'm saving the lemon for dinner. I imagine it'll be refreshing and light. It would probably be the perfect dessert to have after one of those heavy French meals I'm always seeing people eat through brasserie windows.

Not that I'm complaining. I've begun to need only a few bites of food to feel full, to think of exhaustion as a peacefully dozing friend whom I carry on my back. No more worries about the coming night, how I'll get through the next day. Tiny things begin to sustain me: a beautiful umbrella floating above the crowd, the buttery smell of the *boulangeries.* It's warm in the library and impossible to feel poor when I have so many books at my disposal. When the story ends, I sit back and look out the large window that faces the courtyard, three levels down. I see Asad.

Though he has just come from the side door, there is already a cigarette in his mouth. He takes out a black umbrella and opens it. He walks away, his quick, shuffling walk, as though he's trying to stub all his toes. He's heading toward the RER B train to the town of Antony;

then he'll take the bus toward the student dorms in nearby Châtenay-Malabry. He's going home, a place I don't have anymore.

The three girls across from me have stopped their whispering to stare; without realizing, I have stood up from my seat. I reshelve my book and take the escalator one level down. I avert my eyes when I pass the terrace where Asad and I met. I go to the ladies' room, back into my favorite handicapped stall, lock the door, and sit on the ground. I remove from my bag the jar of lemon mousse that I'm saving for dinner, turn it around and around in my hands. It's impossibly smooth. How do they get it like that? No lumps or cracks or anything. What do I want to read next? *Damage*, by Josephine Hart. It's about a married man who falls in love with his son's fiancée and loses everything. In the end, he loves her more. They won't have that here. I'll walk across the river at dusk and read it at Shakespeare and Company.

After that, since I can't think of another thing I'd possibly want to do, I decide to kill myself. Tonight I won't let anything stop me, especially not myself.

THE WEDDING OF Prince Charles and Princess Diana was all my mother talked about for days. She watched it live, then again in the evening, all the news clips and replays. She bought any magazine covering the ceremony and, later, the birth of their son William. *People* magazine put him on the cover when he was a year old. I was in third grade.

"You could marry him. See how cute he is?"

"He's a baby!"

"He's not going to be a baby forever, stupid!" Just like I'm getting used to life on the streets, years before, my mother began to embrace the specter of the White Women who floated through the house, seduced her husband, danced in her mind. She began to follow all aspects of the Royal Family, concentrating on Princess Diana and her sons. She even took to watching those BBC programs they sometimes play on public television, which consist mainly of evil butlers, serial tea drinking, and pasty-faced lovers who clasp each other in the sitting room and wail, "Oh, James, we mustn't, we simply mustn't!"

"Can you do this?" My mother stood up from the couch and, despite her weight, dropped a prim curtsey, spreading the flounce on her housedress.

"Why would I do that?"

"It's a curtsey. It's what proper young ladies do when they meet someone important, like the Queen." She had taken to speaking with a posh Kensington accent at times. I took a step back.

"Man, I've got so much homework...."

"Don't say 'man'! Did I raise you to talk like some little nigger?" This was said in her normal voice. "Just try it." She smiled at me, all tea and crumpets again. I bowed deeply at the waist, like I had seen Bugs Bunny do in that cartoon where he played the piano.

"No! Bowing is for boys; girls curtsey. Here, watch my legs." We went through it step by step, beginning with the struggle to get one of my feet to cross behind the other. After several minutes, I finally got it down—though, glancing in the mirror, I thought I looked like someone ambivalent about going to the toilet.

Then my mother directed, "Now, say, 'Good morning, Mum!'" Her accent took on a Manchester lilt. Two tries to get that right. Then I had to do it with the accent and the curtsey at the same time, without falling over. My mother used to make me do it for bemused houseguests, though we never had too many of those. (Shocker.)

When I was ten, she asked me if I liked the name Heather. Heather was a small purple flower that grew in fields. It was also, she gushed, the name for a pretty little blond girl. She started calling me Heather all the time, ignoring such trivialities as my race, hair color, and ensuing facial tics. At first, I would correct her and she'd hit me. Then I'd ignore her and she'd hit me. Finally, I got used to it. But even before I became suicidal, it was always a worry of mine: *If I die before my mother, which name will she put on my headstone?*

EVERYTHING GOES SMOOTHLY as soon as I resolve to open my eyes and stop ignoring the message fate is bending over backward to communicate: that my only path in life is death, that I must become the Nike of suicides and *just do it!* already.

I spend the evening at Shakespeare and Company, a small independent bookshop; space heaters hum inside the narrow aisles, and an invitingly aloof cat patrols. I finish the final page of *Damage* just before the kid on duty announces the store is closing for the night. For my last meal, I drift over to my favorite bridge, Pont des Arts, sit on a bench, and take out my little jar of lemon mousse, savoring each bite that I eat slowly with the spork I got from KFC.

As much as I try to make my endgame a pleasant one, I can't stop myself from thinking. How could Asad not have known I would end up like this? I'd had to borrow €5 for the Métro from him the day I'd pretended to meet Jamie in Paris. If a person asks to borrow 150 bucks, it means they don't have a lot of money. If a person asks to borrow five bucks, that means they don't have five bucks. He must have known I'd be out on the street with no place to go. He had to know what it had done to me the last time. I tell myself this as I twirl the empty mousse jar in my hands, trying to kindle up a fiery rage.

But what else could he have done? After all, I came to Paris planning to get rid of myself, too. Maybe his only fault was that he was better at it.

ONE THING'S FOR certain: My funeral will definitely not involve an open coffin. Judging from the glimpses I've had of myself in the darkened shop windows I pass, my hair looks like shit. It's rained all day, and my bangs have frizzed into Medusa-like coils that the wind blows about with a persistence it's hard not to take personally. The circles under my eyes have deepened into caverns. I hurt all over now, whimpering each time I hitch up my pack or step off a curb. In the hour I circle the river, not one guy hits on me.

This time, as I walk up and down the Seine, I'm taking measurements. I know the river isn't deep enough to drown in, and where the railings along the sidewalk look over cobbled walkways, the drop never looks steep enough to kill me, only hurt. Bad. If I jumped, I would just lie there, stupid and broken. Tourists would pass me tomorrow and take pictures. I think of hanging myself with my belt or finding a piece of broken glass and slashing my wrists, after which I would hold them in the river. But there again—the pain factor. Life *is* difficult.

I sigh and see my breath. My heart leaps. If I tried to freeze to death now, I really could do it. It'll take me no time to fall asleep tonight.

On the right side of the river, on the Quai de Hotel de Ville, I find a construction site, abandoned for the day. It's fenced around clumsily with waist-high barriers and various planks stacked in piles. I move one, and a mouse scampers out and into a traffic cone. Well. I'm certainly not going to kill myself next to a mouse. I keep walking.

Not too far away, there's an entrance to the river that slopes down, wide enough for cars. From where I stand, I can see another construction site. I watch. Nothing creeps in or out. It's just a still place by the dark water.

As I start toward it, I remember a movie I saw once, called *Afterlife*. It was a Japanese film about what happens to people after they die. According to the movie, we all go to this sort of celestial holding pen, until we can think of a memory, one time when we were perfectly happy. After we do, we go to Heaven, living inside that moment for all eternity. Most of the people in the movie, if I remember correctly, end up living in some moment of their childhood.

So where is my piece of forever? Have I ever had a time, just one, when all was right with the world?

IT'S A WONDERFUL LIFE!

CH. 18

E very Christmas, we made two promises to ourselves:

1) We would not wait until the last minute to get our tree, like losers.

2) We would decorate our tree with subtle, classy ornaments, so it would look like the trees that we saw in the windows of Rich People's Houses.

Christmas more than made up for Thanksgiving, a holiday of which I have two memories: the gelatinous gurgle of the cranberry sauce my dad slid onto a plate from the can, and extended family members crouching down to me as I scratched my legs in my itchy tights. They would issue such conversation stoppers as, "My, you're getting big!" and, "How's school? Fun? I bet it's fun! You're in fifth grade now, right? That must be fun."

The year I was ten, the season kicked off with the delivery of the Sears Wish Book, filled with page after page of every toy imaginable, followed by the ensuing fight to the death between my brother and me over who got to read it first.

"Stop acting like assholes!" my mother would gently entreat. "You think Santa brings toys to little assholes?"

My letters to Santa were more marketing tools than lists. I would include not only the item number of each toy I wanted, but also the item number and a guaranteed sell: "Please bring me a Sony Walkman so I can listen to the radio without pissing everyone off."

Stewie was more adept at kissing Santa's rosy ass and would often pause to read to my mother what we had written: "Please make everybody stop fighting all over the world and love each other and share." He would raise large, guileless eyes to my mother, accepting the kisses she showered on his head.

"Faggot," I'd whisper, when she'd gone back to watching her soaps.

"Santa knows you said that. He knows everything," Stewie whispered back.

"Then he knows you're a faggot."

We would bring home lovingly crafted works of Yuletide art. (This was back in the days when you were still allowed to say the word "Christmas" at school.)

"This is my life now," my mother would say, yanking open our book bags and pulling out green construction-paper trees and red stockings with our names written on the top in glitter. "I should be gazing at priceless works of art in the mansion I share with my rich Italian lover." She glared at the glitter, which had snowed all over the living-room rug. "Instead, I've got every art supply Crayola has ever made, cut up, colored, and shoved up my ass."

"I want my paper-plate snowflake hung up on the fridge," I'd tell her. She'd let her head drop into her hands as I ran to the bureau. "I'll get the tape!"

Every year we would wait until Christmas Eve, like losers, to get our tree. My father had a knack for finding jobs at companies that went out of business or laid off half their staff within six months of his walking through their door. Then the car would break down. And every month, those envelopes with the little windows would come in the mail. I'd see my dad hunched over the dining-room table, staring at them, his tea growing cold.

"Why don't you open 'em up, Dad?" I'd suggest. "Maybe it's good news."

"Yeah," he'd chuckle, "maybe, kiddo."

A week before Christmas, the corner of the living room that was reserved for the tree was still empty.

"All the other kids have their trees already," I said over dinner.

"Yeah, all the udder kids," Stewie echoed.

"We'll get our tree soon, guys," my dad promised Stewie and me as we pushed our tater tots around on our plates.

"When?"

"What's more important," my mother snapped, "a tree? Or all those fucking toys you both asked for?"

Stewie's eyes grew big. "But I thought Santa maked our toys."

I looked at my father. He had raised his eyes slowly to meet his wife's. "He makes them," my dad began carefully, "but . . . we . . . it takes him a lot of time, and we can't get the tree until he sends me a letter saying everything is ready. Right, Mom?"

He hadn't taken his eyes off my mother. He wasn't looking at her the way he usually looked at us, or even the way he looked at the envelopes with the windows in them. This was different. The only sound for a moment was the Coke fizzing in each glass.

"Right," my mother said, glancing at us before looking down at her plate. "Your dad should be getting that letter any day now."

"CHRISTMAS WAS THE best time of year when I was little," my dad told me once. "My mother would go through the house singing. She hugged us. She hugged us enough to make up for the whole year." He sighed. "I always felt like a kid at Christmas."

On Christmas Eve, we got stuck in last-minute shopper traffic, and I worried that the only tree left in the whole wide world (Route 22, Union, New Jersey) would be as pathetic as Charlie Brown's. It seemed like my fears were to be confirmed as we pulled into lot after lot, manned by grouchy, grizzly guys who wore only jeans and flannel shirts, despite the frozen night. ("Aren't you cold, mister?" I smiled up at the more attractive ones whenever we got out the car. They smiled back at me. My father grabbed my hand.) All the good trees were gone, and the only ones left were too skinny or small or lost a disturbing number of needles when one of the workers pulled it out for inspection. We drove on, increasingly silent.

What were we looking for every year? The biggest, lushest, pine-smellingest tree we had ever had. A tree that would make my father forget the grind of bills, dead-end jobs, and the death of whatever dreams he'd had before us. A tree that would make my mother forget that she was in her twenties and trapped in a tiny apartment in the ghetto. That she had a husband who made no money and two children who insisted on talking during the important love scenes between Luke and Laura on *General Hospital.* A tree that would make me forget that I was so chubby, I had to get my jeans in the Pretty Plus section of Sears and cried like a baby every time I got a spanking, no matter how hard I tried not to.

I don't know what my brother wanted. He didn't make a sound until we found our tree in the very last lot we looked in—an unwieldy green monster that took two of the cute tree-lot guys and my father to strap it down to the trunk. Then, Stewie started to sing: "Silent Night" or "Winter Wonderland," everything to the tune of "Jingle Bells." If he was unsure of the words, he'd just add "fa-la-la-la-faaa-la-fa-la-fa..." until we were all singing, more relaxed now that Christmas would happen for sure. Rather than taking the highway home, we drove through the streets, gawking at the homes and front lawns ablaze with colored lights, giant figures of reindeer and candy canes perched like sentries in the snow. Stewie and I danced behind our dad as he wrestled the tree up our building's three flights of stairs to force it through the narrow door of our apartment. We helped our mother take out box after box after box of Christmas ornaments. (The ones we had made in school had mysteriously disappeared.)

We went for classy first. My mother sat on the couch with the first of many glasses of wine while my brother, father, and I hung the imitation-wood snowmen and nutcrackers and elves on the big tree. Then we hung some small balls—colored but still classy, only blue and white. Then we sat back on the couch and studied the tree.

"Can I have a sip of wine?" I asked my mother. My father said no, and reminded me of my age. My mother held her glass toward me and whispered when my father wasn't looking, "Just a sip."

While I took great, violent gulps, she said, "Well, those decorations look nice, but they're kind of swallowed up by the tree. Maybe we need a few more."

Out came the bigger balls, every shade of the rainbow, which, though they were made of a kind of silky synthetic material that unraveled determinedly throughout the years, were never replaced. Stewie and I filled the low branches. My father, sipping wine my mother had poured him in a rare demonstration of wifeliness, did the top. Those balls didn't quite suffice either, though, so we added the shiny glass ones that we always forgot were breakable until somebody broke one.

After that, no point in not using the garlands, both gold and silver, which my father draped about the tree as I drank from his wineglass. The final touch was the tinsel, which Stewie and I did alone and was the most fun—loose, silvery strands that we threw wildly on the tree until it looked like it'd been icicled by a vengeful god. Meanwhile, my mother would make eggnog with dark Bacardi rum—tall glasses for my father and her, a tiny one for me.

"The lights, Daddy! We need the lights!" My father strung the lights while I finished the last of his wine and started on my eggnog. He capped it off with the star, a big golden one encrusted with imitation rhinestones.

Finally, we turned the apartment lights off and the ornament lights on and stared at our blinking, riotous, gaudy, shiny tree.

"It looks so tacky!" my mother giggled into her eggnog.

"It looks like ours," my father sighed, snatching his eggnog away from me.

"We have the best tree ever!" Stewie crowed.

"This is what Christmas is about," my mother said, looking at each of us in turn. "All of us together, just enjoying . . ."

"Can't we at least open one lousy present now?" I yelled, thoroughly drunk.

"Shut the fuck up," my mother said softly, the flickering lights of the tree reflected in her eyes.

IT
HAPPENED
ONE NIGHT

CH. 19

I keep looking behind me to make sure no cars are following, but the streets are deserted. I unbutton my jacket as I walk. "It's no big deal," I reassure myself aloud. "It's just your soul leaving your body. It's just a trip to a better place."

Headlights. I whirl around, yanking my jacket shut like a flasher. A cop car pulls up and three policemen hop out. "Are you a minor?" they ask me. I blink. They sigh. One of them asks me in English.

"I'm thirty." They laugh and ask for my passport. I don't mind. I can't believe I'm thirty, either.

What am I doing out here? I'm so tired and nervous, I get my story confused. I say my parents robbed me and I'm waiting for some gypsies to send me money from a safari. The cops scratch their heads. They tell me it isn't safe here, that I should stay on the inside streets by Châtelet. Their car circles around the block as I head away from the Seine.

Foiled again! I read somewhere once that the reason suicide is wrong is that only God is supposed to decide when we're going to die. I didn't pay much attention to that at the time, but then, I didn't know I was up against such a control freak.

"All right, check it out," I say to God while shivering at a bus stop. "If You don't want me to die, we need to come up with something. I need some sleep. I need some hair gel. And I don't want to have to have sex with anybody for either one." I sneeze, then continue, "Amen."

I think of hopping one of the buses. If only I could get warm, close my eyes for an hour, I know I'd be able to think more clearly. But this time of night, I note, the drivers check that everyone who boards has a ticket. I huddle at the bus stop until dawn creeps palely across the sky, then I head for the Métro. I'm going to hop the turnstile. Let 'em arrest me and throw me in jail; I'll make it in time for breakfast.

I go down to the Quai de la Rapée station. The gates are open only halfway. The station is empty, save a lone clerk behind the glass, head bent over paperwork. I pretend to study the *plan de quartier* on the wall, waiting for the rumble of a train. Then I can jump over the turnstile and catch it before anyone can catch me. No train comes. I go to the station across the street. There are two ticket agents there, laughing about something behind the glass. I go back across the street. The guy from the first ticket window is coming up the stairs, clutching his paperwork. I watch him cross the street and go down into the other station. I run back into the first one, which is now empty. I still can't do it; I can't jump. But I can't go back out there into the wind, either. I just stand there.

A man with a broom comes out of a side door on the other end of the turnstile. He's whistling. He looks at me and asks in French, "You want to come in?"

I nod. He does some clicking to the service gate, and it opens. "*Merci!*" I call to his departing back. Without turning, he waves. I walk down the stairs on shaking legs.

A short guy is walking ahead of me on the platform, a grey case under his arm. A bunch of CDs slip out. I stop to help him pick them up, and we start talking. I'm so gone, my English is as broken as his. He's a DJ, has just come back from a gig. His name is something. For simplicity's sake, I tell him I've gotten locked out of my friend's apartment and that she won't be home until tomorrow. He says his roommate is away; I can stay at his house, if I'd like.

I study him. He's narrow and small and talks in a soft, shivery voice. I can't tell whether he's gay or not. If he isn't, I could take him.

"As friends, right?" I ask. "I just need to crash." The guy nods meekly.

He lives all the way at the end of the line, at Place d'Italie. On the train, I ignore the little glances my little friend throws me. The warmth and rocking of the Métro should lull me to sleep. Instead, my heart is racing. I asked for a chaste place to sleep, and it actually looks like I'm going to get it. True, my hair is still begging for mercy, but I've gotten the most important thing.

I'm jubilant during the long walk to his building, until I ruin it by thinking. First, I wonder how I'm going to make it back tomorrow.

Then, I think, back to *where?*

I've done everything I can to make myself dead, and the only thing that's certain is that I'm not real good at it. I know that sounds ungrateful, that there are so many things in this world to be thankful for: puppies, rainbows, sex. But I wish I could have a sign, something only for me. It's true I haven't succeeded at killing myself, but that doesn't mean I'm supposed to be alive.

There are bunk beds in the apartment's one bedroom, just like the guy said. I slip off my coat and sink under the covers. He goes into the bathroom and takes a shower. He comes out and stands next to my bed, shivering in tiny white briefs.

"Aren't you going to sleep?" I ask meanly. He scampers up the ladder. He turns off the lights. He asks if I'm sure I don't want to cuddle. I tell him I'm quite sure. He tells me he has to be up at ten. It's six thirty. I say that's just fine.

To be in darkness that isn't cold, to lie softly under a warm spread. I wake once, just as the sun is coming up, missing Asad with such an ache. I realize I'm sleeping all the way on the right side of the bed, my hand resting where he would've been.

I shift back to the center. I force myself. Then I go back to sleep.

In the morning, I hurry into the bathroom. The guy is already dressed, waiting for me to leave, grouchy because I've refused his second offer to cuddle.

I pee a trickle, check my face. The caverns underneath my eyes have reverted to regular dark circles. In the mirror, I spot a big white tub behind me. I whirl around.

Gel. Paul Mitchell. The good stuff.

As I'm walking out of the guy's apartment, a bus pulls up to the stop on the corner. I hop on. Ride as close as I can to Châtelet. Hop off. No big deal.

I'm crossing the bridge that will take me to Pompidou, when I realize where I am. It's the same bridge that I limped across the day I met Bertram. When I paused because walking hurt so much, looked into water so black I couldn't see God.

I see Him now, in every miracle: the cops appearing out of nowhere, the Métro worker letting me through the gate for free, some guy taking me home so I could rest and that guy being five feet tall and afraid of me, a free bus ride, super-clean sculpting gel. Maybe one or two of these could be chalked up to coincidence. But, added together, the details of last night are too big to be ignored. I had my chance. I've had a bunch of chances. And every time, something has gone wrong. But people kill themselves all the time—some of them on the first try. What's my problem?

It washes over me like a wave, the realization that it's not a problem—it's life. And no matter how fucked up or painful or hard or unfair or confusing or just plain stupid it is, this is life. This is being and breathing and thinking and making something out of nothing every day. And I know at this moment that from now on I will hold on to it as tightly as I can with both hands until it lets me go. *So stop thinking otherwise—you don't want to leave this place.*

The sun is shining on the river so brightly, it makes the water look almost blue. Tears are streaming down my face and people see and I don't care.

I don't even put on my sunglasses.

THE MIDDLE MANAGER

CH. 20

That evening, I storm out of Pompidou with a purpose. Obviously, I can't count on being as lucky as I was the night before. However, I need sleep; the little bit I've gotten has made me greedy for more. But enough with these flaky guys—their dubious living arrangements, cheap kebabs, and psychotic rage. If I have to trade myself for some shut-eye, I'm going to do it with class.

I'm going to get me a guy in a suit.

I haunt Invalides, the posh area around the Eiffel Tower. After a few hours of passing almost no one, I begin to suspect that maybe guys in suits stow their mistresses (who shower regularly) in apartments, where they can visit them and be home in bed by a decent time. Maybe you don't get to be a guy in a suit without keeping regular hours.

I've been sneezing all day, and my nose is threatening to run. Very alluring. I fumble around in my knapsack, searching for a tissue. I come up with a folded piece of paper—my letter to Asad. I don't remember what it says. I certainly don't want to relive that night. I open it.

All I wrote was, "I didn't do anything. I didn't do anything," over and over again.

You create your own world. Everything around you is the product of your beliefs. If you want it hard enough, you can have it. Some of the richest men on Earth have brought themselves up from nothing. You are here for a reason. There is no one on Earth like you. You are a child of God, with all His powers. You must demand all good things in life. Demand them. Visualize to realize. Just do it. Fear and pain are just figments of your imagination. Your mind is your servant, not your master. Poverty is an illusion, just like the darkness. Turn on the light, and the darkness vanishes. If you're crying in a library bathroom with your scarf in your mouth so no one can hear you, it's your fault. You're doing everything wrong.

The hostel where I stayed! Certainly they'll remember me. I was back there not even two weeks ago, when Asad said I could pick up my luggage. I'll go back, tell them my story. Maybe the truth. Well, at least a better story. I'll offer to let them hold my passport, like Frankie did in Saint-Denis. I'll beg and plead and cry. But I'm sleeping somewhere tonight.

As I turn around and start to walk toward Gare du Nord, I feel strange. While I don't want to have sex with anyone, I long to be held—to be kissed and stroked and caressed and cradled to sleep in someone's arms. Maybe that's asking a bit much. Most married people don't even get that.

Just as I'm passing the Assemblée Nationale, I hear someone say, "*Bonsoir.*" I glance behind me. It's a guy in a suit! He pauses until I've caught up with him on the bridge.

He tells me, in near-perfect English, that he isn't usually out so late, but he had a meeting with some very, very important clients. It went very, very well. I tell him this is my first time in Paris. He asks how I like it. I tell him it's so beautiful, I'm practically dying.

Why am I out at this hour? he asks when we get to the number 1 Métro.

"I don't have any money, and I've been walking around for a few days. I was on my way to a youth hostel to beg them to let me stay there until I could get some." I yawn. "Why?"

He stops walking, so I do, too. He's a big, square man with glasses and a schoolboy haircut. He looks more German than French. His fingers tug on the lapel of his jacket.

"Listen," he says slowly, "when I take a woman home, it's just for fun, just for one night. I don't want to be responsible for anyone."

"Don't worry," I reassure him, "I can take care of myself."

HE LIVES IN Neuilly, a moneyed suburb just outside the city. His apartment isn't very suitlike—just a studio with magazines stacked all over, laundry drying on a rack in the center of the room. But it's warm and his bed looks big and soft. He gives me some sweats and I take a long, scalding shower. He offers me a glass of wine, which goes down very well, having nothing but those two little jars of mousse for company. His laptop catches my eye.

"Mind if I check my email?" I ask casually. If he says no, I decide to murder him with my bare hands, but he turns it on and goes into the bathroom.

I have thirty-seven messages in my inbox. I haven't written anyone since my second day with Asad. At first, the subject lines are "What's up?" and "Bonjour, kiddo!" Soon, they turn into all caps: "I'M WORRIED!" "WHERE ARE YOU????" I almost feel like I'm being held right there. I write everybody that I'm broke, that I need a loan. That if they don't help me, I'll have to start sleeping with people for money. Just joking, I add.

"MY WORK IS in sales." The big man sits on a stool, facing the bed, where I sit cross-legged, struggling not to topple over into sleep. CNN flashes atrocities in the background. "I sell office supplies to big corporations. I have a very high position, even though I am young. When the president and the chairman want something done, they come to me. I tell the little people to do it." His shoulders slump like two ski slopes.

"So, you're a middle manager?" I say.

"Is that what you call it in English? Is that good?" he adds quickly.

"Well, it's not bad. It's like . . . in the middle."

"It's a great deal of responsibility," he says loudly, sitting up straight. "When the salesmen have a problem, they come to me. When something goes wrong, the big bosses count on me to fix it. I practically run that place. My apartment is too small." He gets up quickly, pours us more wine. "And I pay so much for it because it is close to La Défense [Paris's financial district]. This is not quite what I planned on when I was younger."

"What did you want to be?"

"I don't remember," he shrugs. "I'm very unhappy." I sip my wine as he stares at me dolefully. Am I supposed to say something sympathetic here? Really?

As if he's read my thoughts, he begins to chuckle. "But then, look at what is going on with you right now. That is much worse, no?" He laughs harder, slapping his knee with a thud.

Finally, he turns off the lights and we get into bed. "Welcome in France," he says. After three glasses of wine, I find this hysterically funny. He laughs, too, then turns me so that my back is to him.

"Uh…"

"Oh, no, nothing like that. I just don't like for the girl to face me. It makes me nervous. I like to relax first, see." He begins to stroke my back and shoulders and breasts. Behind me, it's obvious that he's trying frantically to bring his soldier to attention. Some condoms lie on the nightstand, looking bored.

I feel the tension roll off me in waves as he rubs my sore muscles, my weary flesh. Finally, he whispers, "I think you are tired. We'll try tomorrow. It is more important that you rest."

"You're a nice guy," I murmur. He puts his arm around me and I fall asleep.

In the morning, after another backrub (more frenzied, fruitless jerking behind me), Guy in a Suit decides that the most important thing is that we get to where we are going on time. He says I can have some breakfast while he showers. In his fridge he has bread, cheese, butter, a package of shredded carrots in a lemon sauce. I have a big plate with a cup of tea. The gel reactivates in my hair after my shower. I use his deodorant. I'm ready.

He pays for my ticket and we ride side by side on the train, silent as all the other passengers. "Next stop is mine," he whispers to me, sighing. "I think this is the worst part of my day." He leans forward to kiss me. I hold out my hand. He shakes it, then disappears into the crowd.

"Hi, I stayed here a long time ago and then I moved in with my boyfriend but things didn't work out and now I have no place to go and no money but you could hold my passport until my parents get back from vacation in Kenya a week ten days tops okay?"

The man sweeping the entryway of the hostel stops and leans on his broom, surveying me with sharp, dark eyes. I just know he can see everything: my following a stranger for €30, my sleeping under a bridge, Asad shoving me away from him, my lying down in the woods to die. He points to the registration desk.

"No English. You go there."

The girl at the desk remembers me. "Do you guys have any room?" I ask.

"Probably." She opens her book, runs her finger down the columns. "No."

God only knows what my face looks like, even with my sunglasses on, because she adds quickly, "But sometimes people call and cancel, or just don't show up. Then a place opens."

"Oh." I let out a sigh. "Does that usually happen?"

"Almost never."

The only thing I can do, the girl tells me, is wait. Maybe someone will cancel. She asks me if I want coffee. Coffee costs €1.30. How could someone have €1.30 just to spend on coffee?

The café-bar on the hostel's first floor doubles as the common room. MTV plays on a set overhead, the videos drowned out by the stereo. Snoop Dogg—one of Bertram's favorites, I think.

I sit at a corner table, watching the place fill up. For the uninitiated, a youth hostel is a place for backpackers to get a dorm bed in a shared room and meet fellow travelers. The tables are crowded with fresh-faced kids breakfasting on baguettes and Nutella, poring over battered copies of *Let's Go.* I realize how lucky it is that I didn't come here last night, when I was desperate, half-crazed with exhaustion.

"Hey! Anybody know what the date is?"

"It's the twenty-first." I've been here nineteen days.

"Who wants to come with us to see Jim Morrison's grave?" a couple of girls ask the room. All these happy people, excited to greet the day. The world looks different to them. They're going to leave Europe with pictures and funny stories, maybe a couple of pounds heavier. I'm going to have flashbacks, ribs that stick out like hoops on a barrel. As far as stories go, I'm certainly not going to get any out of this.

"IT'S NOT FUNNY!" I yelled. I burst out of my mother's room as though I'd been launched. It led right to the kitchen, and there I stood, shaking and furious amid the cheerful farm animals that adorned every available surface. My mother almost never left the house now, had taken to decorating and redecorating every room with frantic whimsy. Martha Stewart wasn't even around to blame yet.

"Oh, get the bug out of your ass. I was just joking," my mother called from her room. "Maybe if you had a boyfriend, like normal sixteen-year-olds, you wouldn't be so damned uptight about everything."

Friday night was indeed when most of my friends were out on dates. This was my cue to burst into tears and spend the rest of the night in my room. Maybe right before he went to bed, my father would knock on my door and set a cup of tea on my dresser, leaving with his eyes lowered so he wouldn't have to see mine.

"Fine!" I yelled instead. "Maybe I'll go out and get one. Maybe I'll go out and not come back." I turned and ran down the hall. As I did, it was as though the weight of all the years flew off me. I had loads of friends with whom I could stay. The only days I didn't cry were the ones I slept over at other people's houses. Imagine several days in a row, whole weeks even, without crying. I could put pepper on my food without getting grounded for acting like a nigger. I wouldn't be called "pathetic little virgin" and "whore" in the same breath. Maybe I'd stop being so nervous around guys. Maybe I would get a boyfriend.

I started throwing clothes into a suitcase. I threw in some books from the top of my dusty desk. All my friends were good students. Maybe I'd turn over a new leaf, start doing more homework. Or some.

"Oh, hell no!" my mother roared, bursting out of her room. I heard her lumbering down the hall as I tried to close up my bag. The zipper had caught on one of my sweaters. My father called from the living room, "Um . . . what's going on?"

My mother filled the doorway. "What the fuck are you doing?"

"I'm leaving. I hate you. I'm leaving."

"You're not going anywhere."

"Yes, I am."

"No, you're not."

"Yes . . . " This could go on for a while. I stopped talking, slung my half-open bag over my shoulder. I walked up to where she blocked my exit. "You don't treat me right. All my friends' moms, the ones you see in books, on TV . . . you don't act like other mothers. You don't act like other people at all."

My mother took a deep breath and looked at me. Then she stepped aside. I was on my own. Once I left, she had told me since I was six, I would never be permitted to come back. I would have to drop out of my college-prep classes, go to school half days, and work a job in the afternoon, like the kids from the bad side of town. I didn't care. At that moment, the world seemed as wide and boundless as . . .

Then she screamed. My mother threw back her head and issued such an unearthly howl that my father came running and my brother shut and locked his bedroom door.

She charged. I threw up my hands, but it wasn't me she was after. Still screaming, she dove toward my dresser, sweeping off the jumble of cosmetics and hair things. She ripped off the snapshots and the *Far Side* comics and the peace beads on the mirror. She ran to the walls and yanked off the poster of the Harley-Davidson my best friend, Alex, had given me for my birthday and tore to shreds the *Simpsons* poster my friend Jen had painted for me in watercolors. She yanked drawers completely out of the dresser and sent hangers spinning through the air. The center of the room became a mountain of dismembered stuffed animals and torn clothes. I stood not frozen, but warm and wet, as the pee ran down my leg in a thick stream. Only when it stopped could I jump on the bed and grab her hair.

"Stop it! Stop it! That's everything that's mine!"

"Nothing is yours! Nothing!" My mother turned to hit me, and I clocked her one in the face. Then I jumped off the bed and ran to my father.

My father responded by pushing me onto the ground and smacking me over and over on the thigh. His eyes were big and scared. He had never hit me in my whole life. When I was little and wouldn't eat my oatmeal, he'd say, "I bet you can't finish it before I fall." Then he'd stand on his head. Now he was holding me on the floor and beating me while my mother ripped and tore and smashed.

Suddenly, everything stopped. My father stood up, turning this way and that, as though he didn't know where he was. My mother stepped over me, picking her way delicately through the debris.

"Oh, leave her, John. If she wants to go, let her go. The bitch is crazy anyway."

I didn't clean my room for two weeks. I didn't move permanently out of my parents' house for ten years.

COFFEE AND CIGARETTES

CH. 21

T he common room of the hostel soon empties out: People clear their breakfast things off the tables and hitch up their day packs. They leave in chattering groups, shielding their eyes with their guidebooks as they step out into the bright morning sun.

I try to keep my eyes glued to the overhead TV, both so I don't notice the increasingly pitying looks the receptionist throws me and so I don't stare at the sole couple in the corner. They're slumped over their table, their bodies limp commas of hangover. They look happy, though, sipping their little cups of coffee, sharing the same cigarette. Try as I might, I can't help but think back to about a week ago, when Asad and I broke up in a café and I thought he'd left me with nothing to lose. And how, suddenly, I realized that as far as my being left with nothing, that had happened years ago.

The café was so close to the dorms that I could see them from the window across from our booth. Asad ordered us coffee, got us a pack of Marlboros. He explained things as I smoked them one after the other.

My suitcase and my overnight bag, I had a week to come back and get them; else he was going to throw them out. If I tried to come back to his room later that day, or for any other reason than to get my stuff, he would call the police. When I was ready to get my stuff, I was to email him. I was never to call.

"You don't have to do it like this, you know."

"Like what?"

"Like you're enjoying it. You don't have to look like you're having so much fun." His eye twitched twice, as though it were flirting. He lit a cigarette.

"You will find someplace," he said through the smoke. "Everybody has it hard when they come to a new country. I myself, believe it or not, had a very difficult time. When I came here, I found things were much harder than in Tunisia. There, I was the best in my classes. Here, I was just in the middle. Still, I could've gone to the top engineering school if I'd wanted, but I chose this one, where I am at the head of my class." He stared at the ashen curls of smoke rising from his hand. "I can't stand to be in the middle. If you are in the middle, you are lost." He was the third of five children.

"I just don't understand," I whispered. "First you said it was fine that I leave on Friday. Then you said I had to leave tonight and come back in the morning because you were going out and didn't want me alone in your room. Even though," I added, "I've been alone in your room every day for two weeks. It doesn't make any sense."

"Don't talk to me like that!" he snapped.

"And now you're making me leave right this second. I can't go back out in that cold, Asad. I just can't." I started to cry again, burying my face in my hands. I heard our cups being picked up. Asad ordered two more coffees.

"I don't owe you anything, do you hear me? I owe you nothing! I took you in as a *geste humanitaire* ... "

"Oh, really, Gandhi, would you have invited me to stay with you if I was ugly?"

He looked affronted. "I don't sleep with ugly girls. Look at this, speaking of ugly."

I'd left a moon-shaped scratch on his wrist.

"Well, look here," I showed him the one he'd given me on my thumb. As we compared wounds, our hands almost touched.

"I'm kicking you out because you make me nervous. You don't shut up. Why don't you shut up? Why don't you shut up when someone tells you to shut up?" When begging and crying and insults hadn't worked, I'd tried to get him to hit me. I'd followed him, I'd grabbed his hand, I'd shoved the back I used to nuzzle, until he'd turned around and knocked me on the bed.

"Get away from me! Don't stand too close to me!" He'd backed away from me, practically sliding against the wall as I collapsed upon the bed, before the pile of clothes I'd have to pack all over again.

"I don't care what you say," I sobbed. "I know you loved—"

He heaved a big sigh, looked at his watch.

"Okay, okay, forget it. Just . . . not yet, okay?"

"Finish your coffee."

I took an obedient sip. It burned. "Five more minutes?" I pleaded. He sighed again, nodded.

I hated myself then, of course. I knew if I didn't have him, I would die. If I didn't have this person who treated me like shit, I would die. I couldn't explain it, but it didn't feel wrong. It was the most familiar I'd felt since I'd stepped onto the plane at JFK.

"I wish things didn't have to end like this."

"It doesn't matter, as long as they end." As he said this, he didn't look at me. If he had, he would have seen my mouth drop open, the flush of recognition.

Of course. I was being punished! I had come to Paris to die. God had let me come here, and then I'd changed my mind. I mean, yeah, suicide is a sin, but a promise is a promise. Things weren't going to get better for me; they were just going to get worse—steadily worse. Any good times I'd had were a distraction, a setup for the inevitable.

"You're right," I said, feeling stronger. He shifted in his seat so he could look at me without seeming to. "It's better that this ends, all of it. I pick the wrong friends. I've never kept a job longer than nine months. I don't talk to most of my family. All my relationships with guys suck. I never have any money. I didn't make it as an actress. I dropped out of college. I never finish what I write. I've failed in everything. My God," I whispered. "They should put my face on a penny."

"What? What does this have to do with us?"

"I just wish things could've been different. I wish *I* could've been different. I wish I had my own little place and my own money, and we could've met like normal people and gone to the movies and talked on the phone. I wish I'd met you back when I was still okay. But then, I guess you wouldn't have gone out with a four-year-old."

He blinked, signaled to the waiter for two more coffees. "I don't follow you."

There were seven cigarettes left. We'd been there for two hours. "If I tell you something . . . no, I'm *going* to tell you something. Because it doesn't matter anymore. I've never told anybody. Not even myself. But only because I know you're not going to see me again." When I put a cigarette in my mouth, he leaned over and lit it, his eyes on the flame.

"All right. Tell me."

"When I was little—well, starting when I was little—I think my mother molested me."

He shrugged. "Everybody's mother molests them."

I had forgotten: Arabic, French, *then* English. "No, I don't mean *molester*, like, 'to bother someone.' I mean . . . never mind."

"No, tell me! You have to now."

"Forget it, it doesn't—"

"Tell me, or I'm leaving."

I looked down. The coffees had arrived. They gave us only one sugar cube on each saucer. Asad didn't like sugar, so I'd been taking his cubes and he'd been letting me. It was like we had an understanding.

"I mean, she touched me. You know, she touched me where she shouldn't, like the way a guy touches a girl."

He sat straight up and stared. He put his legs up on the seat, pushing himself back. The table we were sitting at had two chairs facing a long, wraparound booth. He was in the latter, now stretched out along the cushions, arms folded across his chest.

"I don't understand."

"Forget it, then."

"How did she? Why did she? What did she do?"

"I just told you."

"No!" He shook his head angrily. "What did she do?"

The sugar cube was perched upon my wet spoon, dying as I spoke. "Starting when I was about five, she would call me into her room. I would stand by the door. I would put my hand on the doorknob. Even in the summer, the doorknob was always cold. She would be laughing. She would say, "Come on. Come over here. Be brave." When I would come over, she'd hold me down. And when I screamed, she would ignore it. When I tried to fight her off, knock her glasses off or something, she would hit me and send me to my room. Sometimes, when she was done, she would hold me down and open her mouth and hold it open until her drool fell on me. If I tried to get away, she would tell me that if I moved, it would just come out faster."

"Where was your father? She did this when he was working?"

"Not always. Sometimes he would stand outside the door (she'd always make me close the door), and he'd say, 'Dana, please don't do that. What are you doing? You can't play with the kids that way.'

"When I got older, she'd grab my breasts and shake them. If I got mad, she'd say they weren't mine, that she'd made them. Once, she did it and I got so mad I tried to run away. She trashed my whole room."

"You told me ... " The seat made a hissing sound as he slid down in the booth, stretched out full-length. "You told me you have not spoken to her for two years. Why did you stay so long?"

"I didn't remember. Or, I mean, it was all my life, you know? I didn't connect it with anything real, anything that had to do with her. It always seemed like my bad. One day, when I was twenty-eight, I was visiting and I noticed she had hung these art postcards on her wall, female nudes. I made a joke about her coming out of the closet. She blew up, started yelling at me, calling me all kinds of names. Then she goes, 'Why would you say that? Is it because of something I used to do to you?'" I dunked the cube into the coffee, but it'd turned into a lump, clinging to my spoon.

"Even right after that, I couldn't think. I couldn't make sense of what she said right away. How could I make sense of something that didn't make sense?

"But I'm not blaming that for the way I am. Tons of people, you know, get messed with. A lot of Bosnians got gang-raped. Or was it Serbs? I don't know. But you can't blame one little thing for your whole life.

"It's not an excuse. It's just a reason. I've never worked very hard at anything. That's why I don't have shit. It just seems like it's not worth it. Like everything's going to get taken from me in the end. I don't know why I think that. Nobody ever *stole* anything from me. I had a shitload of toys when I was little ... "

He sat up again, stiffly, as though he were rising from a coffin. "Be back," he muttered, walking quickly to the bathroom.

I looked around the diner. Two old men were watching the TV at the bar. A man in another booth was reading the paper over a basket of croissants. Our waiter was cleaning a table up front, swiping the crumbs onto the floor with a rag.

I'd done it. I'd said the end-of-the-world thing, and the world had kept going. Even if it was going to end for me, nobody else was going to be affected. They were all going to be okay. Even Asad, who somehow managed to look both pale and flushed as he returned from the bathroom. Everything was going to be okay.

As often as possible, my father took me with him on errands. The minute the car pulled out of the drive, we'd explode with jokes and puns, political commentary crafted specifically to incite the other person. We'd drum on the dashboard along to songs on the radio, stuff ourselves with sweets like orphans at Christmas.

One evening, pulling into the driveway after a trip to the market, he pointed to the lawn. "Check out how the grass looks caught in the headlights." We both stared at it, the way each blade held itself straight and still beneath the glow.

"Sometimes," he sighed, "life almost seems special." For a moment, my father's face was hidden in the shadows. Then he turned off the lights completely.

A pig appeared as I put the last cigarette into my mouth: a little pink lighter with a curly tail. It belonged to our waiter, an old man with kindly eyes. He didn't know what was going on, that I wasn't some heartless bitch torturing a young boy, some crass *américaine* stomping on the heart of a sensitive Frenchman. He'd just seen a woman crying. He lit my cigarette, then handed the lighter to me.

"Oh! *C'est* . . . how do you say 'cute' in French?" I looked at Asad, who lifted his head slowly from his arms.

"I don't know," he whispered.

"*Merci.*" I smiled at the waiter. I kissed the pig and handed it back.

THE
LITTLE
FRIEND

CH. 22

I t takes me almost three weeks to try to die in Paris. After I decide I don't
want to kill myself anymore, it takes me seven months to get home. I
am nothing if not efficient.

And in those seven months, I do what's aptly known as "crashing."
Thanks to the kindness of the expat friends I make at the hostel, I crash
on narrow beds and lumpy couches and mattresses on the floor and
sometimes just the floor, and not once in all those nights do I forget that
I am not out in the cold, and on each of those nights, as I lie down, I feel
that I'm sinking into the biggest cloud in the sky.

The days can be a bit harder. I have to do a lot of odd jobs, some
odder than others, for not much money, and try to save as much of that
money as I can so I can get back to my old life, which, as you'll recall, was
so unfulfilling that I fled the country to escape it. And while I'm working

one of those jobs or looking for the next, it's always in the back of my mind: how I can make things work when I get back home. How I must.

Maybe that explains the fantasy I have most nights when I go to bed. Actually, I'm not sure whether it's a fantasy or a dream, since it usually continues as I fall asleep. Either way, it gets me through the night. It consoles me for the morning.

I dream I go back in time to our old apartment and meet myself when I was a little girl and steal myself away.

But it's more complicated than that. The dream is always about the same day: the day my mother and I walked through the storm. In my head, I take my mother away from the window and sit her in front of the TV, where she was usually to be found. When I walk through the front door, my brother is still in his playpen. My father is still in the bedroom at his desk, poring over the classifieds. I see my four-year-old self staring out the window, and I move in that direction as quietly as I can. I know the others can't hear me or see me, but that's not why I don't want to make a sound.

I always choose the stormy day because it's the last memory I have before the abuse started, and I like to think of myself then. I used to try to think of how I would be now had it never happened. But I couldn't imagine it, so I gave that up.

You HEAR ME behind you. You turn and smile. You're always glad to see me because I take you fun places, even though all the while I give you a lot of boring advice you don't understand. Your liking me comes as a surprise. The first time I came to visit, I thought you'd be afraid. I thought you'd turn your back on what I had become.

You raise your arms so I will pick you up. You are wearing over-alls because that's what Dennis the Menace wears, and underneath, an orange T-shirt that says 99% GENIUS, 1% ?. This is your favorite shirt, because your daddy bought it for you, because it's not pink, and because even before you know what they mean, you love question marks.

The pockets of your overalls are lumpy with Brach's candy wrap-pers, and your fingers are sticky with either Welch's grape jelly, Oreo crumbs, or M&M's, the latter of which, bewilderingly, melt in your mouth *and* in your hands. On your four pigtails are four mismatched barrettes. You lose the matching ones when you shake your head side to side as hard as you can, because sometimes you are a helicopter. One overall strap or both are twisted because you rush on your way out of the bathroom, just in case you're missing anything. When I pick you up— your warm, undamaged weight—I think, *How could anyone hurt you?*

But that's a silly question. How could anyone hurt anyone?

To get out the door, we'll have to walk by our mother, slouched on the couch. I want to get you away from her as quickly as possible. But something always makes me stop. Makes me watch the shadows from the TV advance and retreat across her face—the face of a twenty-four-year-old who will never go to college or on spring break or on a road trip with a carload of friends. Who will never have a honeymoon or struggle to nap on the red-eye coming back from a business trip or travel cross-country for a friend's wedding or back to her hometown for a high-school reunion. She'll never need a passport or vacation anywhere more exotic than Orlando. And someday soon, maybe tomorrow or next week or next month, the most restless woman in the world will begin to call you into her room and will very nearly guarantee that for the rest of your life you will never stop running.

I know I should hate her. Don't worry, I do. Closure is for politicians and talk shows. But I also can't help but wonder.

What happened to her? Who did it? And where did that person go?

When we step outside, we'll be in Paris. But it'll be spring, with soft, warm air and blossoms on the trees. After all, Cole Porter didn't write a song called "Paris in October," and in a dream, at least, you can have anything you want.

I always take you to the Champs-Elysées, because you like the Arc de Triomphe and the happy crowds and the big McDonald's. I always let you buy something at McDonald's so you won't get homesick. But unlike when you're at home, I hand you the money to pay.

You have to learn how to deal with money. By the time you really have to, you will have gotten so used to living in denial that you'll close your eyes to anything that proves to be the least bit stressful. But money doesn't bite. Unless you don't have it. That really bites.

Back outside, as you skip beside me, spilling french fries along the Champs, I continue.

A guy will treat you only as well as you treat yourself. If he's not capable of treating you the way you deserve to be treated, run, even if he's hot. Especially if he's hot.

Don't look for your employees to adopt you. Don't expect strangers to take care of you. Don't let what anyone tells you take the place of your brain and your gut.

We go to Châtelet. You like the young, energetic atmosphere, the street stands, the street dancers. We also pass the street people: the dirty, the wistful, the crafty, the rebels. Perched anywhere and everywhere, begging passersby for change.

It won't always be easy, especially the way you will be raised, but don't judge people on superficial stuff, like race or class. And don't worry about those who use those criteria to judge others. Just work on being the best person you can be, and you'll attract the same.

At this, you look up at me and frown. You point to someone in the crowd. It's a mime.

All right, I relent. You can judge them.

And speaking of other people, there are those who will notice the cracks in your happy-go-lucky act and will want to help you. Mrs. Whidby, for one. Also your fifth-grade social studies teacher, who will ask you if you need to talk, after your losing a strawberry-scented eraser sparks an hour-long bout of weeping. ("Nah.") Your Spanish teacher sophomore year will note your silence and make you stay after class to ask if everything is all right at home. ("*Sí.*") Your unappreciated guidance counselor, Mrs. Peniston, will keep calling you into her office, nagging that you need to think about your future. You won't be able to ask her how in the world you can, when the present is almost more than you can bear.

Then, because this is all getting a bit heavy, I take you to the Jardin des Tuilleries. I let you sail boats in the fountain and watch you run in and out the flower-lined paths. I don't say anything at all.

By nightfall you're getting tired, but it's important that I take you to the Eiffel Tower. I want you to see how lovely it is when it glitters, and how lovely are the upturned faces that watch, because it's the only way I can try to make you understand that life is so much more than just what happens to you. Can you understand that? Will you remember? Time to go back to the bridge? Okay.

The worst part is when I have to take you to the Seine and leave you at the bridge that will take you back to the past. Because I know what's going to happen to you at home. And that it's going to obscure what's good out there in the world. And that through all the heartache and mistakes that go along with such a perspective, you'll believe, in your heart of hearts, that there's something wrong with you. That you're intrinsically bad. And you'll spend hours, years, watching the people who seem to have it all together, studying them like textbooks, then hating yourself for failing every test life sends your way.

Listen, this is important: Suicide is like a terminal disease. It's like a virus that turns your mind into a mad dog and then yells, "Sic!" I don't know if it goes away for good, or just into remission. But you have to learn to stay away from situations that could trigger its return. You have to learn how to fight if it does. When it does.

And just remember, that's what Mom wanted: to make you as crazy as she was. If you commit suicide, you'll be letting the terrorist win.

You watch me, unblinking, unmoving, but starting to slip away. The floor of the bridge where you stand has begun gliding backward, like one of those moving walkways at airports, like the very earth is pulling us apart.

As you move away from me, I shout, "And just for the record, you don't talk too much! You don't need too much! You're not too much!"

And there's one more thing, but I don't know what to tell you, because I don't know what to do myself.

To my surprise, the bridge stops. You're still halfway across it. But you can hear me. I take a deep breath.

Your friends are going to say, "But why don't you talk to your mother? You have to talk to your mother. Everyone's mom drives them crazy." They'll say things like, "You should have heard the nasty remarks my mom made about my hair the other day. I mean, I *cried*, but I didn't stop *talking* to her."

And your family will say, "Your mother misses you, sacrificed so much, lived her whole life for you kids. . . . "

"Besides," everyone will add, "You have only *one mother.*"

"And halle-fucking-lujah for that!" you'll want to scream, though you won't. But don't get mad at them. How could they know?

But one day, you'll get sick of hiding and you'll have to tell them, and that's the part I'm not sure about. I don't know how to tell anyone what happened to me.

You walk back to where I stand. I bend down as you reach me, the better to hear you say, "This is how."

Then you put your hand on my cheek. I've forgotten my hand was ever that soft. And as I watch you turn and walk back across the bridge, all I can think of is what a nice kid you are, and how I hope the world lets you stay that way.

HOME

CH. 23

"Hi."

"Hi."

"Hi."

Three kids stand in front of my table at the hostel: bright eyes, shower-damp hair, each clutching a beer, though it's barely eleven in the morning.

"Mind if we sit here?" the girl chirps. The breakfast rush is over; I look pointedly at the empty tables on the other side of the room. They sit at mine and start laughing full force, as though they've deactivated the pause button on a previous conversation.

"So, she believed you?"

"Next time we saw her, she was at the ticket booth, arguing with the woman about a refund."

"Americans are so stupid."

"Hey…"

"I can say that. I'm American."

"I thought you were Canadian."

"Why would I be Canadian? And you guys are the idiots. You know what they did to some chick from Palm Springs?" The girl turns to me.

One of the boys starts laughing again, waving his hand like he wants to tell it.

"Whenever we meet somebody on the train," he tells me, "and they're all excited about going someplace for the first time, we tell them stories just to fuck with them. We've been everywhere."

"Twice," the other guy pipes up.

"They're Australian," the girl tells me. "When they travel, they drag it out for years."

"It's because we're so far away from everything," Jason retorts. "At least we see the world, unlike Americans."

"Yeah, you guys just eat the world."

"Thanks, have some beer." The girl dips her fingers into her mug and flicks some at them. The boys dip their fingers into their mugs and flick some back. The girl flicks some more.

"So, what do you tell these people?" I interrupt, taking off my sunglasses to dry them.

"Oh yeah. For instance, we meet this woman and she tells us she's going to Paris for the first time. 'You boys have to tell me all about it!'

"So we look at each other and start shaking our heads. And I'm like, 'Paris ain't that great. Especially the Eiffel Tower. What a disappointment!'

"And the woman's eyes get all big, and she's like, 'Whatever do you mean?' And we're like, 'Haven't you heard? It's all rusty now, and broken. They give you hard hats if you're going to walk around, because pieces of it keep falling off.'"

The other kid breaks in, "'And the elevators are broken, too. So if you want to go to the top, you have to climb up all three thousand or so steps. When we were there, a little old man collapsed and people kept walking over him.'

"We told her the Louvre is shit, too. That France needed money, so they sold all the good paintings to the Japanese. And they put up posters over the empty spots.

"So the woman's like, 'Maybe I'll just go to Milan and shop.'"

"Aren't they terrible?" the girl asks. Laughing makes the muscles in my stomach feel like they're stretching after a long night's sleep.

"My name's Lindsay, by the way," the girl says. I introduce myself. So do Matt and Jason. They study me over their mugs.

"You look hit," Jason observes. "Lemme guess: You just came from Amsterdam."

"No! A massive pub crawl in London."

"I know! You took one of those sleeper cars from Prague, and you were afraid of getting gassed and robbed, so you stayed up all night."

I'm dying to put my sunglasses back on. "Actually, I've been in Paris for a while."

"Not here. We would've seen you."

"Yeah, we know everybody."

"I stayed here my first night. Then I ran out of money, so I walked around for three days. I ate only once a day and hardly slept at all, except for one night with some squatters under a bridge. Then I met this guy and I moved in with him for two weeks. I really loved him, I think. But he thought I was cheating, so he kicked me out. I walked around for three more days, until I couldn't stand it anymore. I've just given them my passport to hold at the front desk. I emailed my friends, asking them to send me money. Maybe they will . . . I can't really think about it right now."

I begin counting the seconds until I have the table back to myself. The three kids sit back in their chairs. They let go of their mugs. They look at me, then at each other, then back to me. The kid named Jason clears his throat.

"Dude, you need a beer."

SOMETIMES YOU WAKE up in the morning and have no idea it's going to be one of the best days of your life. Lindsay is from San Francisco, the boys are from Perth. Strangers a week ago, they've formed the fast and easy friendship common among travelers. After my speech, I return to being dazed to the point of muteness, the perfect audience for all their anecdotes. Plus, they like a girl who can hold her beer. After my third, the room starts to swim pleasantly. Some angel of God puts a bowl of peanuts on our table.

"Excuse me, girl in the trench coat." The receptionist is waving to me. "We have a room cancellation. You still want it?"

I stand up. "Listen, guys, I think I'm going to take a nap for a few days. . . . "

Jason pulls me back down. "What do you want to sleep for? You're in Paris!"

My new friends have been only to the Latin Quarter and the Eiffel Tower, so I show them all around Châtelet. They love Les Halles, the secondhand shops and street performers. We sit by the fountain behind Pompidou, the one with the colorful ducks and hats and giant sets of lips spewing water all around. In addition to Métro fare, they treat me to a crêpe for being such a good tour guide. We each have a different kind— sugar, chocolate, and ham and cheese—and rotate them for tastes.

Suddenly, I think of Luciano. Where is he now? Did he go back to Pont des Arts that day to wait for me? Have things somehow gotten better for him? Food, shelter, kindness—this guy who had less than any- body I'd ever met gave me everything I needed, never asking for a thing in return. And I wasn't very nice to him. I treated him like shit, actually. I never even said goodbye. A wave of regret wells up, the kind that crests but never falls, only follows you around for the rest of your life.

We stop at an Internet café. I think of all the people I wrote, telling them I'm in trouble. They're probably all laughing at me, talking about what a loser I am. To prove their point, I realize that since I have no money, I'm not going to be able to check my replies.

Suddenly, at her station, Lindsay pushes her chair back from the computer. She has tears in her eyes.

"What's wrong? Bad news?"

"Here." She gets up, gesturing to her chair. "There are a few minutes left; don't let them go to waste. I have to make a phone call." She hurries to the call booths behind us.

Everyone has written me back. None of the subject lines say, "Loser."

"Go check Western Union on Monday, God knows they were my best friend when I was in Asia...."

"Take your time paying it back...."

"It's not much, only 100..."; "75..."; "200...."

"Glad I could help. By the way, what the heck are you doing in Paris, you nutty girl?"

I WISH I could say that the money I was sent was enough to get me back to New York. Still, it was enough to allow me a few weeks to recover before I had to start looking for work: to stay at the hostel, to start sleeping and eating every day so that I stopped fainting each time I bent down to tie my shoes.

The money gave me someplace to go when darkness fell, because during those first few weeks, I couldn't shake the feeling that if I found myself outside at night, I would be forever lost.

I wish I could say that I don't know what winter is like when you're twenty pounds underweight and don't own a coat. Or what it is to try to survive in a place that doesn't know you exist. Or that I never again put my well-being in the hands of the wrong people. Or that my taste in men immediately stopped being as healthy as napalm.

But I can't say that, because happily ever after doesn't exist for people like me. If love is blind, then to be abused by the people you love is to put on blinders. And it's when they finally come off that you can really lose your way.

But once they're off, if you find yourself getting off track, you can retrace your steps and start again. At least you can start again.

I DECIDE TO let the hostel hold my passport until the next morning, when I can go to Western Union. I make plans to meet up with Jason and the gang later on, and crawl up the six flights of stairs to my room. After waking from a four-hour nap so delicious it should've had a Zagat rating, I notice that my bunk bed is pushed against a balcony, a narrow affair overlooking a canal, with a knee-high railing all around. It's barely big enough for the four of us and a fat bag of hash to squeeze out onto later that evening. The boys laugh at Lindsay and me, clinging to the windowsill.

"What are you hanging on like that for?"

"It's windy!"

"Yeah, we could die!" I add. The boys scoff and sit on the railing until the hash hits and they start swaying.

"Sit down," I command sternly.

"Yes, Mom." They wedge in between us.

"I wonder what my mom's making for dinner," Lindsay says suddenly. "I checked the weather back home. Rain. On rainy days we always have macaroni and cheese, the real kind from the oven, where the top gets all nice and burnt."

"It's summer in Australia right now. So it's barbeque lunch and dinner. My dad does brilliant prawn kebabs."

"Sometimes when I first wake up, I think I smell my mum's bacon and eggs frying, but it's just Jason's feet."

"I've got two more months before I go back."

"Three weeks."

"I only have . . . hey!" Jason points to our right. We hadn't noticed before, but we can see the Eiffel Tower in the distance, almost as tiny a point of light as the joint we pass. It starts to sparkle. I look over at Jason, waiting for him to say something sarcastic, but his eyes are fixed on it, cold air escaping his mouth like a visible sigh.

After the sparkling stops, the boys get the munchies and leave to get us all some Chinese. When we're alone, Lindsay turns to me.

"Want to hear something stupid? I got this email from my mom. The cat has learned how to unroll the toilet paper. He runs it down the stairs, all through the house; my dad's flipping out. When I read that, I wanted to go back home so bad. I wanted to sleep in my room and eat cereal in the kitchen and fight with my sister. I called my mom and I was, like, bawling for ten minutes." She takes a quick drag of the joint. "Am I an idiot or what?"

No, I think to myself, *you're lucky. You'll always have a place to go if things go wrong, a place where you can feel safe.*

But I'm pretty lucky, too. And I can spend the rest of my life clinging to some person or a fantasy of some far-off place. Or I can make up my mind to cling to myself. On second thought, I guess you don't have to cling when it's to yourself. All you have to do is hold on.

"You're just homesick," I tell her. "Don't worry. It's something everyone goes through."

THE LAST TIME I SAW PARIS

CH. 24

Monsieur Legros, the owner of the English-language school, is counting out my pay. I've just finished a week teaching intermediate conversation to adults. It's been seven months since I've been homeless, and I still can't get over the fact that I have actual paper money.

Of all the gigs I've had, this is the best one, I think, as I watch him count out the pale blue euros. Still, he keeps the €20 bills with which he pays most of his staff in a safe beneath his desk. It's *that* kind of job.

Legros always has a freshly lit cigarette in his mouth, which he never ashes. I'm half-afraid an ember is going to fall onto my pay, setting the whole thing ablaze. Things are different now. Better. But at times, I can't shake the feeling that even the most incremental increase in my well-being could disappear like *that,* could slip through my fingers like a cold night breeze.

"So," Legros says, as he hands me my envelope, "you are leaving us. When is your flight?" He's a big man with a bluff, hearty manner, so disarming that at first I think I'm imagining things when the envelope he hands me feels about half as light as it should.

"Um, in two days. I'll miss it here, but I think it's time to go back to the States. Speaking of which . . . " I hold up the envelope. While I've got a bit of savings, I'm counting on this week's dough to help tide me over while I get settled. It will mean the difference between having to hit the ground running and just hitting the ground.

"What is wrong? Ah, *oui, l'argent.* I am afraid the bank is giving us a hard time. It happens, *pas de problème.* Could we just send you the rest of your money in a few weeks? Do you know where you will be staying over there?"

He looks like he wants to go on, but something in my expression makes him burst out laughing.

"But I am kidding, no? Of course you must have all of your pay." Still chuckling, he plucks the envelope from my rigid fingers, stuffing the rest of my money inside.

"*Mon Dieu,* but you should see your face! And they say the French have no sense of humor. . . . "

The school is housed in a nondescript one-story on a noisy street not far from the hostel. But in front, hidden from the street by a high stone wall, is a courtyard. It is here, after taking my leave from M. Legros, that I sit down on a stone bench and count my pay. Just in case. It's been a long time since euros seemed like play money to me.

When I'm satisfied, I take a moment before leaving. It's one of the things I'll miss most about Europe: the hidden courtyards many businesses have, an oasis of calm between one's obligations and the rushing world. This one is particularly nice: Its cobblestones still glisten from a daily hose-down; lush plants, looking incongruously tropical, grow against the walls. Before I can stop myself, I think, *Wow, if it were a little warmer, this would be the perfect place to sleep.*

I CHASTISE MYSELF about that all the way to the bus stop. I'm meeting some friends at a pub in the Marais for a last night out before I leave. But despite the comfort of having people who care about me nearby, a place to sleep, and work, however sporadic, I still can't stop doing what I call the night watch: where I look at the world as though I were still homeless. I always notice places that stay open all night long. If I find a bistro with self-contained bathrooms, I think, *A person could freshen up and change in here.* Where others might see a cozy nook in a park as a perfect place for a picnic, I see a safe place to sleep or cry. I hoard nonperishable food and travel-size toiletries like I grew up during a depression. Maybe, in a way, I did.

But I have to believe everything happens for a reason. And that includes the way we suffer, and the lessons that suffering imparts to us.

I have to believe that.

STILL, IT'S NOT all hypervigilance and gloom. In the same way I used to look for answers within my past, now I'm always thinking of the future. In fact, when I get to the bus stop, it's almost as if the people waiting there represent the options that await me.

There's a group of multiracial university students crowded on the first bench, sharing one cigarette, talking in loud, exuberant French and poking the one unfortunate among them who's trying to study. Next to them is a businesswoman who's tapping something into a handheld device and giving the students dirty looks. In the middle is a young couple. The man holds groceries in two tote bags, a habit I've picked up since I've been here. The woman looks down at the baby in the carrier she wears, smoothing its sparse hair.

The students fall silent with a sudden hiss, and I look up. Coming straight toward us is a girl with dead eyes. Her walk is slow. It's a bright spring day, almost warm where we sit in the sun. Some of the students have taken off their jackets, loosened their scarves. This girl clutches her thin sweater tightly to her with both hands. I can see how nubby the material is as she draws closer, that her hair is a bit matted beneath the hat she wears. The girl's complexion is the same as mine. She's pretty, or used to be, or could be again, if only her eyes weren't so staring and horrible. She sits down next to me so heavily, she makes the whole bench rattle.

No one at the stop speaks now. Even the students look at the girl with disapproval. They probably think she's on drugs. I would too. But I recognize the flat-footed, painful way of walking that develops when all you do is walk. I know that she sits with her shoulders hunched and her mouth tight because you can get so tired that even the wind sounds like a scream. I wish I didn't, but I know the disbelieving way the eyes stare into a future that doesn't contain a single meal.

Too bad, I think, *she doesn't have any sunglasses.*

One by one, in their polite French way, the people at the bus stop get off their seats, gather on the curb, and make a show of peering eagerly down the street for the bus. The girl either doesn't notice or does a hell of a job pretending not to.

By the time the bus comes, I've finished digging around in my bag to separate some of the money from my pay envelope into a side pocket. I don't want to embarrass the girl by offering it to her here, so when I get on the bus, I will sit in the first seat I can find that's empty two across and signal for her to join me. Then I will ask her, in halting but discreet French, if she needs help. Not that you can rescue people with fifty bucks. But you can buy them a good night's sleep, a meal, give them the strength to save themselves.

I find a two-seater and watch the door. The students shove their way into the back, and the businesswoman sits up front, as far away from them as possible, with the young couple behind her. Then the doors close and the bus pulls up a few feet to the red light.

I whirl around to peer out the window. The girl is still sitting there, staring hard at nothing.

Of course! She's not sitting there to catch a bus. She's sitting there because she's been walking all day and all night and she can't do it anymore.

That's just what you used to do. How could you forget?

I close my eyes and take a deep breath. It's something I'm learning to do, to not beat myself up for every little mistake. After all, I tried. The old me would have gotten up to wait at the curb with the rest of those people, with my back turned, leaving that girl all alone.

Anyway, you still have yourself to worry about. You've got a long way to go. Because for all the effort I've expended trying to figure out how to die, I have the feeling that learning to live will be the kicker.

I open my eyes again to look out the window and mentally wish the girl good luck. When I do, I can no longer see her.

I realize that the light has changed. I've turned a corner.

•

ACKNOWLEDGMENTS

A h, if only I could list all the people who believed in me when I didn't believe in me ... but that would take a whole other book.

I'd like to thank my agent, Jamie Brenner, for seeing the potential in an early draft and giving me a shot; my darling and handsome little brother D.A.T., otherwise known as Pudie, for putting up with his bossy big sister for all these years; my teacher/mentor/friend Cris Beam, for forcing me to write about my childhood when I was like, "What does ending up homeless and suicidal in a foreign country have to do with my childhood?"; Zack Hample, and his wonderful writing group circa 2005–07, for encouraging me to read them this story when I was afraid they would think I was crazy. I was, they assured me, but crazy sells; one of my favorite memoirists, Tommy Pryor, for his continued love and support.

And of course, Kenneth Halpern: No matter how far I travel, you will always be my country.

ABOUT
THE
AUTHOR

© RICAHRD BOLL

After Naturi Thomas finally made it back to New York, she moved twelve times in three years and had twice as many jobs. Wow, she got tired just writing that. She now lives and attends grad school in London. She hasn't wanted to die in ages.